John Albee

New Castle

Historic And Picturesque

John Albee

New Castle
Historic And Picturesque

ISBN/EAN: 9783744733564

Printed in Europe, USA, Canada, Australia, Japan

Cover: Foto ©ninafisch / pixelio.de

More available books at **www.hansebooks.com**

BY

JOHN ALBEE

ILLUSTRATIONS

BY

ABBOTT F. GRAVES

BOSTON
1884

Press of
Rand Avery Supply Company
Boston

NOTE

An islander sometimes forgets there is any other world than that which confines him within its familiar limits. The English and Irish, and other nations, testify to this experience; and it has had the effect of forming distinctive character and history.

The reader of these pages, therefore, must excuse the writer, if, in the concentration of his vision, a square mile of islanded rock appears unconsciously magnified to continental proportions.

It has been an agreeable labor to draw together all that concerns a spot whose boundaries are so fixed by nature, and whose inhabitants, moulded by their environment and pursuits, have had a remarkably uniform destiny. As in your own garden, you know, with a pleasing satisfaction, every tree and plant, so the small area and well-defined annals of this ancient town flatter the investigator with the feeling that he may master them all. But much comes to light after the most careful research; after the book is closed some missing leaf may be found. History must be written before it can be corrected and amplified; to find omissions and errors, we set down what we have collected, and better students will not be slow to discover our deficiencies.

Here I have erected a small column, and have not covered it all with inscriptions; I have left plentiful space, which, in future editions, I hope for coöperation in completing.

NOTE

I wish to acknowledge my obligations for assistance in compiling this little book, to my fellow-townspeople of the older generation, both men and women; to the Hon. Secretary and Deputy-Secretary of the State of New Hampshire, for access to MS. documents: to Hon. Charles H. Bell, of Exeter (N. H.), to Hon. J. H. Trumbull, of Hartford (Conn.), and to John Savary, Esq., of the Congressional Library, for valuable information.

In behalf of the town of New Castle, and of myself, I desire especially to express my obligations to Hon. Frank Jones, at whose suggestion and generous aid this book has been prepared.

I have used freely State and local histories, transcripts of original documents, local biographies, guide-books, and the MS. records and papers of New Castle; also, though often with much perplexity, all the volumes of New Hampshire Provincial and Town Papers.

Most of the seals and autographs have been drawn by J. B. Thurston, Esq., of Concord (N. H.), from original papers in the State archives, in the most faithful manner; the drawing of the New Hampshire Provincial seal is especially fine.

CONTENTS

First Settlement of the Island

Descriptive Walks

Internal Annals

Religious
Civil

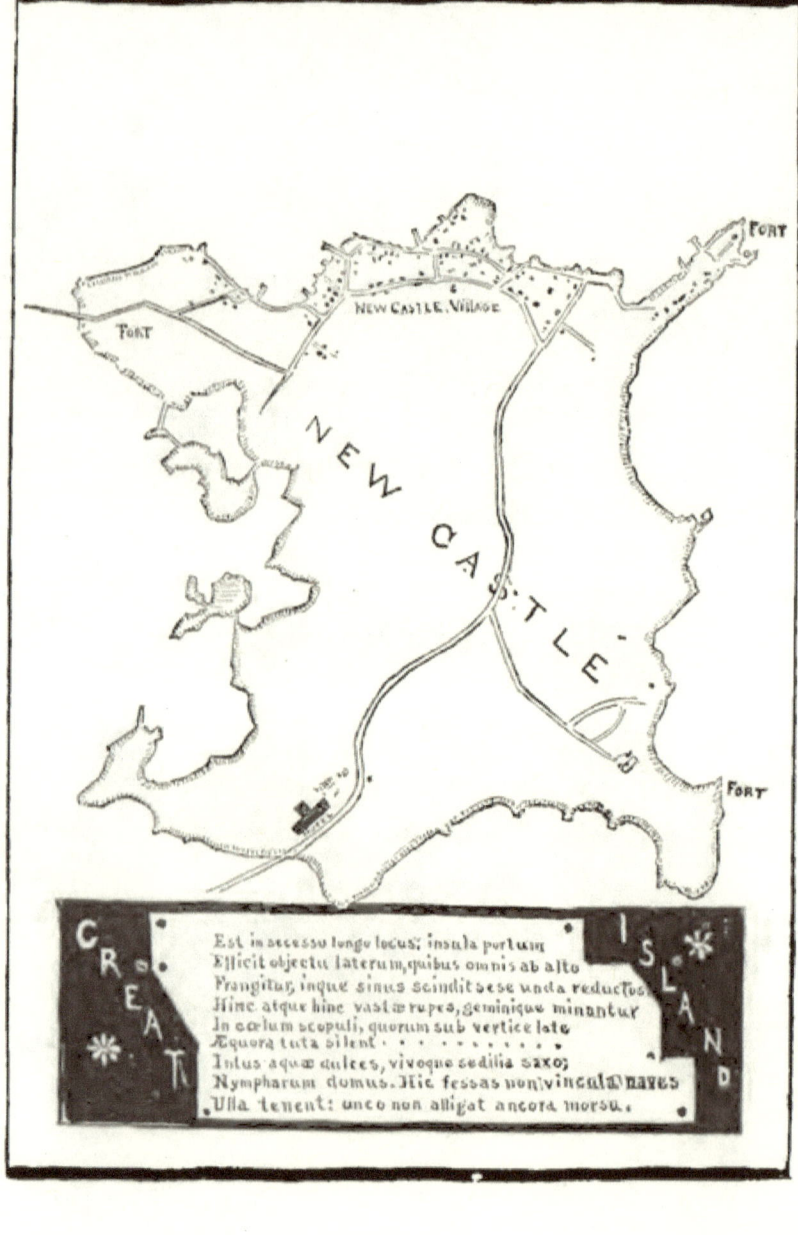

ILLUSTRATIONS

	Page
Mending Lobster-Pots	4
Last Lombardy Poplar	6
"Now which wife was this?"	12
Site of Mason Hall	18
Paul Revere's First Ride	22
Gateway of Fort Constitution	24
Walbach Tower	26
Boatswain Allen's House	28
Jaffrey Cottage	30
The Wentworth	32
Portion of Province House	36
"Here she lost her heart"	38
Captain John	40
Cape Road	42
Site of the Stone-throwing Devil	44
Fort McClary	50
Navy Yard, from Three Bridges	54
Church Point	58
Frost Fields Mansion	60
Whale's Back Light	64
Elm-Tree Cove Cottage	66
Hotel Wentworth and Surroundings	68
Old Wentworth House	70
Mantel of Wentworth House	74
Strawberry-Patch Road	76
Tucker Farm	78
Tucker Farmyard	80
Langdon Farmstead	82

ILLUSTRATIONS

	Page
Rev. John Emerson	102
Interior of New Castle Church	112
Home of the Salamanders	128
New Castle Interior (after Town-Meeting)	138
Our Alley	142
George Jaffrey	144
New Castle Fishermen	154

COINS, SEALS, AUTOGRAPHS, &c.

Old Coin	7
Autograph of John Cochran	23
First Fort on the Piscataqua	29
Comet of 1680	49
Piscataqua Gundalow	56
"Sign of ye Dolphin"	76
Well of Tucker Farm	84
Walter Barefoot's Autograph and Seal	125
Great Seal of Province of New Hampshire	132
Theo. Atkinson's Autograph and Seal	140
Rich. Jose's Monogram Seal	140
Jaffrey Clock	144
Jaffrey Coat of Arms and Seal	144

NEW CASTLE

HISTORIC AND PICTURESQUE.

IN the year 1873, the ancient records of the town of New Castle were discovered in Hertfordshire, England, and not long after returned to their original home. These records begin in the year of the incorporation of the town, 1693, and extend to 1726. The charter of incorporation, on parchment, elegantly written, and with all the legal redundancies usual in such documents, by singular good fortune has never been lost or stolen. It is all whole and legible, though faded and yellow, the proper tokens of its authenticity; only wanting in its royal seal, which some too fond lover of antiquities has abstracted. And now, in the current year, 1884, an antique silver seal,* found among the relics of the Langdon family, has been restored to the town.

With these documents and the references to be found in the New Hampshire Provincial Papers, together with local traditions, the memories of old people, and the general history of the settlement of New Hampshire, it is now possible to collect a few fragments of the annals of New Castle.

In relating this small local history, I am moved by a sense of duty rather than by my tastes or my fitness. In truth, there is no one else who will undertake the labor; and only the accident of my situation has made it incumbent upon me. It is, I confess, a novel situation to find oneself without a competitor; and

---

* A fac-simile of this seal is printed on the title-page.

the reader must not expect those restraints which every writer imposes upon himself when at work in his own appropriate field. I wish to make a picture rather than another document. And I am quite of the opinion of old John Aubrey, the famous English antiquary: "Methinks it shows a kind of gratitude and good nature to review the memories and memorials of the pious long since dead and gone."

Yes; this is what I have felt in reading or hearing the old memorials of this island town; gratitude for the piety and bravery of its forefathers, and only good nature and amusement at their quaint customs and narrow affairs, over which they spread all the dignity and ceremonials of a little kingdom. And the story is typical of what happened everywhere in New England, when men, from necessity as well as choice, put in operation the principles of free government, and bound communities by their self-determined regulations. Thus the social and political history of our country can be read in small as in large; as clearly in the village of New Castle as in the town of Boston. But as the early municipal regulations were strict and minute, and more or less sumptuary, and as they concerned sacred as well as secular affairs, the functions of church and town not yet being divided, some part of the life of the people escaped their stern codes, and overflowed into what we may call the embroideries, or frosting, of their annals. It is these which distinguish and characterize many New England settlements. Time and growth have obliterated them almost universally, and they exist only on record or in tradition. In a few places, untouched by progress, they remained until a late period. These embroideries, that is, those things beneath the dignity of history, must be preserved with the greater care. Welcome are the poet and artist who magically touch what the historian dare not, the unauthentic, the incredible!

The records of New Castle are confined, for the most part, to the barest recital of the transactions of town meetings, the allotment of lands, ear-marks of cattle, births, deaths, and marriages. If this were all that happened in the period covered by the entries, we should have to believe our fathers and mothers lived indeed vapid and unexcited lives. But it is aside from probable fact, for they were pioneer adventurers, not Puritans; islanders, with unknown seas and rivers in front of them, and behind them mysterious mountains and forests. Add, also, the fact that they were, for the most part, of old Celtic blood, from Devon and Cornwall, and of a more imaginative and excitable cast than the generality of New England communities, and there is sufficient ground to believe that life had here a picturesqueness and flavor unrecorded by the town clerk or the parish minister. Within my recollection there were traces of this peculiar insular life; its faint, vanishing odor, like that of an old attic or long unopened book, I sometimes detected when I came fresh from the modern New England. But the summer wave of civilization moves continually eastward, leaving its money and its manners; taking away, in return, health, a stiller nerve, and, if possible, some old china and colonial chairs. The instincts of the people are changed, and a frightful mediocrity threatens every most sequestered New England nook. I refer only to dress, houses and their furnishings, and books commonly found. The unfittest alone survive: the small room, the close stove, the tawdry subscription-book, the frying-pan and bean-pot.

The traditions, habits, manners and customs, and provincial speech of the people of New Castle are rapidly passing away. They have had, in a marked degree, all the peculiarities belonging to people living on an island. Eastward of all thoroughfares and lines of travel, and sharing in that fate which arrested the commerce of Marblehead, Salem, and Portsmouth, they have been left undisturbed for a long time by the so-called progress of the age. Still they have kept to their calling, seafaring, though not of the old kind which took them around the world, and was often a liberal education; but their seafaring has followed the solitary eastern and northern haunts of the cod and mackerel, so that their lives have been still more remote and incommunicable than when at home. Thus their characteristics became strengthened into a type which, though passing, is not quite extinct, even in the present generation. The women still know when one of their companions is lost, before the survivors return to tell them. The sick hold out on the night flood, but die on the night ebb. Nor will pork fry well, but is watery and sputters if butchered when the tide is coming in. The sun, the wind and the Rye rote mean much; and a hundred little happenings make up their current wisdom and daily miracle. Their neighbors' cats, dogs, chickens, and boys, put them into a state of siege and constant declaration of war; yet in the memory of man there has been no great crime committed here, and few, if any, petty. This does not signify a superior state of morals. Morals are ideals, to be exemplified and measured by intelligence.

New Castle is a very compact little village; the houses are almost as near as in cities. Never anywhere could you hear the perfect theory of minding your own business expounded so well and so often as by the citizens of New Castle; but one has a suspicion — how did it become so popular a topic? Blood relationship exists in this community to an astonishing extent. Everybody is related to everybody; and very likely the person you are speaking ill of is first cousin to the person you are addressing. Inter-marriage has been almost of necessity, since the inhabitants seldom went abroad and few strangers settled here; and this has helped maintain the characteristic features of the town without apparent physical degeneracy. The chief and almost sole variation in the local strain of blood, has been introduced by the bold soldiers who have garrisoned Fort Constitution at different periods since the Revolution; these, and an infrequent, stranded seaman, have produced the only irregularities in genealogy. So fondly attached are the people to their island that they cannot live elsewhere, save at sea, without homesickness; and if any strange, upland man, happens to marry a New Castle woman, he must make his home here, and love the town with an undivided heart, if he wishes domestic concord and contentment, and a town office. Fond, local attachment belongs to dwellers by the sea. Nor can they be happy away from their boundless horizon.

"Illusion dwells forever with the wave."

It is their constant excitement and stimulant; their wonderland no less than their larder and support. It is their almanac and clock; by it they mark most natural phenomena, measure their toil and rest, their riches and their poverty. The mariner and fisherman know the perils of their calling, but enjoy the struggle, lead an alert and boisterous existence, and are happy; often improvident; experiencing more than most men the frail tenure of life. Mountaineers have much the same attachment to their homes, but are more sombre and apathetic.

You cannot climb the summits every day, and at length they deject and conquer puny man. A mountain is a noble neighbor, a river is a pleasant companion, but the sea is a master. It is good to abide by; emblem of activity, of mystery and eternity. It draws the boy from the shore and makes him a citizen of the world. He loves it as a plaything, so easily moved and still so smoothly strong, fascinating and graceful, yet perilous, "the woman of nature;" and it is the child's fondness for water that later has made him use it for his trade and profession.

But the New Castle sailor, if he outlive danger, gladly returns to his birth-place, and like the Kenites of old, "puts his nest in a rock," and falls easily enough into its circumscribed life. It is impossible not to admire a people who have maintained, from the earliest times, their unity, traditions and blood; who are as far west as they wish to be; and in a restless age, have kept the path their forefathers trod.

It naturally might have been expected that the close proximity of Portsmouth, and dependence in many ways upon that city, would have produced some noticeable effect upon New Castle, and involuntarily have carried it along with the times. But there has been a rivalry in ignorance of each other between these two populations, so naturally connected, and, in fact, formerly one in their interests and affairs. They have not known each other for some two generations; and Portsmouth did not re-discover the island until pointed out and adopted by strangers. It must be taken into account, I suppose, as a partial explanation, that since 1812 Portsmouth has been herself in a state of decay or paralysis. Her activity has not been overpowering to the surrounding towns. She is not aggressive or grasping; she has little of the missionary spirit, loves to be well let alone, and impresses the observer as needing nothing to complete her perfect and serene self-satisfaction. This, with her well-preserved colonial architecture and long-descended household furniture, china and silver, and the gentility befitting such inheritances, as well as that which comes of breeding and ancestry, make up the chief charm of Portsmouth. The tranquil streets, the clean, comfortable appearance of all externals, and the completed and restful look of everything, make one grateful for the fate which has left it undevastated by improvements. But i' is a long time since Portsmouth held any social relations with New Castle. Some of her most distinguished families in old days, — the Sheafes, Atkinsons, Jaffreys, Vaughans, and others, — came from New Castle. The only occasion when the citizens of Portsmouth take much interest in our islanders is on election anniversaries. Formerly the town election was held just one week previous to the State election; and it was the only local election in New Hampshire occurring so near the general; and this happened in conformity to the ancient charter of the town. In times, therefore, of political excitement, a fierce contest always occurred over the election of town officers, as their political complexion was supposed to indicate the general result in the other parts of the State. As goes New Castle so goes the State, was the current saying.

Emissaries from Portsmouth and other parts of the State, with well-filled pockets and oily tongues, used then to labor diligently among us, and made us believe we were of vast importance and the best fellows in the world. We were welcomed in Portsmouth as persons with the destiny of the country in our hands, and the great men of our little metropolis couldn't see enough of us. Of course we were flattered and swelled to the size of the party balloons. We made feasts for them, we and our wives and children, and then we all made speeches, saying the cleverest things we could think of in each other's praise. It did seem as if the lamb of Great Island and the lion of Strawberry Bank were about to lie down together; or, in plain language, that now we were of the size of Portsmouth, and that intercourse and good-fellowship would no more be interrupted. Alas, it was all very bad for our morals and politics, and especially unfortunate in the administration of town affairs, which became of not the least consequence when party questions intervened. We were periodically neglected, and for a few weeks petted and cajoled by the customs officers, postmasters, and great statesmen of Portsmouth. This is now all changed, in the change of the State election to the fall of the year; and the local affairs of New Castle are at present well managed and generally entrusted to the best men, irrespective of party prejudices. Some grievances remain, a legacy from the period I have described. Among them, a war debt of twenty-six thousand dollars, now bonded at five per cent; as unjust and undeserved a burden

Last of the Lombardy Poplars.

as ever was inflicted upon any community. The levies of soldiers for the war of Rebellion were made upon a fictitious basis of enrolment of more than thirty per cent. But we bear it without flinching, have always paid the interest promptly, and some portion of the principal; and, meanwhile, have never curtailed our appropriations for schools, roads, or other public interests.

The very isolation of which I have spoken, has made the people self-dependent, and their enterprise has been adequate to their necessities. They built the first bridge of any extent in the State, over Little Harbor, for their own convenience and that of their outlying townsmen in that part of their territory now called Rye, and formerly Sandy Beach; they built the first mills, saw and grist, damming the tide for supply of power into the same reservoir now used for the small pleasure-boats of Wentworth Hotel. The present dam is built upon the foundations of the old. Here, also, is said to have been in old times, a bakery; and on the shores near the supposed sites of these buildings, led by dreams and traditions, people still dig for buried treasures. This search for gold and silver, hidden by pirates, or when the ancient settlers feared the coming of enemies, has been a frequent incident in New Castle annals. Seldom, however, has it been undertaken by natives; they know better, and can, any leisure day, with a couple of dories and a windlass, fish up in the harbor an anchor or two, worth more than all the treasure-trove yet discovered. The next best thing to do is to dig in one's own garden; there are certain riches which come to the surface nowhere larger or more abundant than in the fertile bowls of dark mould between the warm ledges, which run northeast and southwest across the island, dipping at an angle of about 45°. Yet I will not deny that several interesting relics have also been found, as coins, Indian implements, and some of our grandmothers' spoons, crocks and buttons.

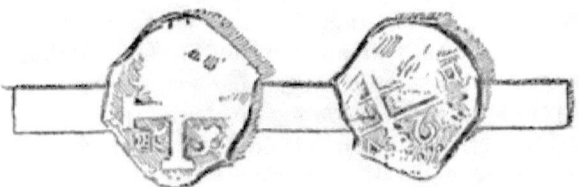

Human bones would be more common did we dig deeper; for every field has been a burial-place in times gone by, when the dead reposed in their own acres, and were comforted by the near presence of their beloved homes and unforgetful friends. All over the island, singly or in families, sometimes with a marble or slate memorial, sometimes with only the rough stones of the field planted at the head and foot of the low mounds, rest the lofty and the lowly forefathers of our present villagers; rest amid the ledges, where the thin soil scarce covers them warmly, or yonder in the edge of the field, where the ground is not too precious for other planting; there the tanzy grows rank, and everything betokens the consecration of neglect; there the ancient gravestones lean and crumble, the names grow dim and become to the living like the names of strangers. Yet however bleak and desolate the situation, the ocean is everywhere in full view. Nor could one seeking where to rest when his watch was over "wish for couch more magnificent."

Whether our ancestors derived the custom of selecting the most barren soil for burial-places from the ancient Britons, who appropriated the moors and waste places for a similar purpose, is a matter of conjecture. Certainly it is a most ancient custom, practiced by many nations, and the Egyptians buried their dead in the desert. Plato, in The Laws, would forbid food-bearing ground being used for sepulture, and assigns only useless spots. And he also adds an injunction worthy of being repeated to ambitious monument builders: "Make not the upright tombstones greater than what may contain the praises of the deceased in *not more than four heroic verses.*"

But only a part of New Castle's dead sleep in their native earth. Some are at the bottom of the stream which empties here; some in the Eastern bays, and many in those waters so fatal to fishermen about the Georges Banks. One cenotaph in the town, records the loss of eleven men, in the prime of life, in the space of eight years. The inscription reads:

> "To the memory of the citizens of New Castle lost at sea. I saw the dead, small and great, stand before God — and the sea gave up the dead which were in it."

As I have said, though only a part of the dead are here, the ground is full of graves. One of my old neighbors who owned a yoke of oxen and did most of the ploughing in town, was always in fear lest his cattle should sink a leg into some ancient grave, as had often happened. By this sign he knew where many of the old family burial-places were, even though the ground was level. "I've been in them," he said; "in old times they didn't dig very deep, and when the coffin gets empty and the wood thin and a heavy ox steps on the right place, down he goes." Sometimes we plough up a couple of wedge-shaped stones, like colossal Indian arrow-heads, near together, in the line of the same furrow, perhaps; we know very well what they signify, and haw the cattle on the next bout. Between them, according to that lamented scholar, poet, and Portsmouth antiquarian, John Elwyn, "sleep the early settlers, full of years, labors, simplicity, and — rum."

Very likely, for in the last seven years of the last century, nine men and two women, Lucrece Tredick and Grace Yeaton, retailed rum and other spirits to the thirsty citizens, going and coming from their labors, their dry sermons, wet funerals and jolly weddings. This was at about the rate of one rumseller to every fifty inhabitants. How much have we changed since those dear, sad old times! And now there is no liquor sold in town — and the wells give out almost every summer: Last year was exceptional; at the laying of the corner-stone of Mr. E. C. Stedman's tower, we had an excellent punch, composed by the poet and his architect, which carried us comfortably through the dry season.

But to come back to our mortuary annals: once only can I remember that we turned up a slab of slate having a name and inscription. We laid it aside on the top of a ledge, and there it remained for a long time. No one knew anything about it, or the name and dates, cut deep under an urn and weeping-willow tree. Now, because our town records are uncommonly complete and go far back, the descendants of old New Castle families often come here hunting for their ancestral tree. Not often do they find much more than names and dates. But one lucky gentleman, a somewhat distinguished sculptor, not only traced his family record here, but recognized the stone I have spoken of as his remote ancestor's, reclaimed the forgotten memorial and carried it off in pious triumph to adorn the wall of his studio in Florence.

However, I would warn all explorers after their genealogical tree, that we cannot always furnish such tangible mementos of their progenitors; it would be like expecting the college of heralds not only to furnish a coat of arms, but plate and coach.

Within a dozen years two attempts have been made to enclose a public cemetery in New Castle. One of them was a failure, owing to the fact that its projector was one of its first occupants; the other has been a success, and, so to speak, is the fashionable resort. It is very well situated, sloping to the western water. Both were private enterprises, for the sole end of money-making. If anything could be queer in this trading world, it is the making merchandise of sepulchral ground. The poor man is seldom able to buy more than what would be the corner of a potter's field; and he never would be rich enough, after the expense of a lot, however deep his grief, to erect a tombstone large enough to contain four heroic verses.

It is already sufficiently difficult to live in this living age; but who can afford to die? Only the rich, and members of the New York Stock Board with their ten thousand dollar premium on death. Let us have cremation as a way of economy, but not cremation companies; that also has the taint of profit and loss. Let every man have his own ustrinum, which is easily made of flat stones, a cord or two of good fuel, a little oil, sweet spices and a few pieces of wood whose combustion emits a fragrant smell, like the black birch or apple tree. Then gathering up the small remains, they can be affectionately deposited under the humblest roof, there to abide honored and incorruptible. "He that hath the ashes of his friend, hath an everlasting treasure."

One of the consequences of our popular cemetery in New Castle, has been the removal to it of the scattered dead from private grounds, sometimes in possession of their friends, more often not. It is disturbing to one's sensibilities to see his dead reposing in another man's field; they seem but half his; they seem to reproach him with some indifference. But this digging up the long buried dead is a dreadful trade; a curse is upon it from of old, either through honor or hate. Better they should slumber where the first thought placed them. Nature will honor them when men have done. She wreathes a testimony out of their neglect. I love to see the scattered, sequestered graves in the lone and waste corners of our island. There the wild rose, the bramble, the tanzy, and perchance some garden flower, struggling for life through half a century, gather and grow with a more profuse luxuriance and a brighter color. There let them sleep.

Perhaps the reader will think this is but sentiment, and that, at any rate, we have tarried long enough among the dead. But he must remember that New Castle contains eight generations of dead and only one living; and though I did not promise a faithful history, we must find our perspective in the past in order to group intelligently our modern figures and manners. I will only take the reader to one more graveyard, that of the colony which first settled New Hampshire and built Mason Hall. But before doing so I will describe a scene, at which I, in a manner, assisted, and which forever prejudiced me against the removal of dead bodies from one place to another.

It chanced that a very aged man, who once had lived in Jeffrey Cottage, and from thence had buried, long ago, his helpmeet in a field belonging to it, bethought him in his latter days to gather into one place the several wives whom he had lost and buried in his various wandering homes, so that he might be laid himself, at his own soon-expected end, beside them all. Thrice had he been mated; now all were gone before him. His earliest mate was here; and here, one gray, autumnal day, he came to disinter her remains, then thirty-two years under the turf. There was no fence, no stone, and scarcely a mound to mark the spot. The field had been ploughed, but the grave still maintained a slight elevation above the level, so that the plow respected it, and the long grass had grown uncut, ripened, and fallen over it in a tangled mat. The old man brought with him a grave-digger, who was the brother of Hamlet's. He removed the turf gaily, and as fast as the spade went down his spirits rose. I thought it forced, to encourage his own fearful heart in the ugly labor. The old man sat in the wagon close beside the grave; he was too decrepit to do more. To him the grave-digger addressed most of his grim and not too delicate sallies, of which the old man took no notice. He did not answer, he did not speak; his sad, dim eyes were looking out over the dim sea. It was fifty years ago he was looking into. The grave-digger was in no haste now, after he had cut through the tough, bound-out turf; he too, ever and anon, leaning on his spade, gazed at the sea; then put in his spade again, and presently remarked that he thought he had "struck her;" queried of the old man, how much he expected to find of her; and "was she a good sized one?" "Women goes quicker 'n men, 'specially if they're plump." "Now, you, old man, will last a good long time after you are laid in; when a man gits down to the bone afore he dies, he has a good chance of stayin' pretty much so — till he's wanted — which is n't often. Women does n't come diggin' up their old hubbies, no, I guess not, not much; they goes flipperin' around after a live one." "Is n't that so?" and he winked at the old man, who paid not the least attention. "Now, which wife was this? Lem me see — three — this must have been the first woman; well, you'll make quite a company when we git you all histed out and laid in a row long er the old man — and most of the children dead, too. What a dreadful dyin' lot you've been, though."

At this cheerful remark the old man turned to me and inquired what I got for my potatoes this year. It was a faint attempt to change the subject, to divert his own mind, perhaps to dissemble his pain. I sympathized with him and pitied him; but was, I confess, too much absorbed in the whole spectacle, which realized to me more than I had ever seen before, on or off the stage; and whose pathetic and comic aspects, there in the desolate field beside the lonesome sea, never can be forgotten and never portrayed — until I assist in the long expected "great American Drama."

The grave-digger was now removing the top of the coffin, grown thin as veneer, but without a rent. I peered fearfully down, attracted and repelled at once by the ghastly expectation. The clown looked up and asked if I supposed I should see any worms. I said no, I thought they must have finished their contract. "Meetin'-house talk, young man; minister's lingo. There

"Now which wife was this?"

ain't no worms where dead folks be; they's as pertickuler as the rest on us; they knows what they likes, and this ere sort of sugar would n't melt in their mouth; nor they don't never go nigh so deep, they'd be dead themselves first. They goes 'bout as deep as a plow, not a mite more, and don't care to tackle the underpinnin' of the airth, let alone yer mohugany coffin boards, silks and satins and them air best clothes old folks used to dress up their corpses in. They don't like no such things, these ere common worms runnin' roun' the ground. Good 'nough meetin'-house talk; but the fact is, young man" — here he held up a lock of hair fastened to a soft, half fluid clot of black dissolution — " well, if I had this ere job of callin' sinners to repentance, I could give 'em some pints wus than worms. Look at that air stuff! would n't they go for'ard lively for prayers now, if you could just picter out the raal state of the case in about thirty years' time after they warnt no more livin'. Them's the pints I'd give 'em; and I'd stock up our old empty meetin'-house till you could n't get a back seat with yer gal. Them as has been down into a grave knows how things air down here; and this ere talkin' of worms and dust and ashes don't alarm nobody who don't know how it is n't so."

In some doubt as to where this last statement had landed him, he added, reflectively, " It's just so." I nodded assent, wishing to keep him from tantalizing the old man. But it was in vain. Having delivered his little science to me and his scheme for awakening the unconverted, he returned upon his victim.

" Shall we scrape her all up, old man ?" " All," said he. " Well, commonly, folks is pretty well satisfied with the bones. They think they've got 'em when they've got their bones. I tell 'em they're 'bout right. Bones is e-nough, e-nough; the rest on us might as well be in one place as 'nother. We shall git a new settin' out by the time we want our bones agin. Howsumever, old man, we'll git her all together, if you say so; mebbe she was precious.

" Young man, just pass me that box; the old man is so slim i 'spose he could n't git out of the wagon if 't was his own funeral." The grave-digger, seeing we neither of us smiled at his jibe, chuckled himself audibly. I handed him a small, plain box from under the seat of the old man's wagon; he took it and set it down in one end of the grave, remarking to me in a whisper that it was large enough for a whole family of *undergrounders*; and that he should put in some dirt with the remains, "so the old man shouldn't be disappointed with the small lot of his first wife." Then he lifted out the box and clambered out himself, refilled the tenantless grave, hammered down the cover of the box with a stone and placed it back under the wagon-seat.

Then they rode away together, the quick and the dead; he to his old, she to her new abode near by, where she might more conveniently await his coming, which, it seemed to me, was now the only wish of the pious and venerable old man.

I could not feel, after this strange scene, that he had robbed me or my fields of any of our dead. There remained no less to them and to me. And the triviality of the grave, even its humor, the thought of which the irreverent grave-digger had provoked in me, was quickly silenced as I walked home past a spot of newly mounded earth. The grave-digger himself made the whole scene so unimaginable and fantastic, that in a little while I was in doubt whether it was actual or a dream.

New Castle, being situated between the two outlets of the Piscataqua river, must have been naturally noted by the earliest navigators; but is not mentioned by any name which we now recognize. Martin Pring, in 1603, explored the Piscataqua for ten or twelve miles inland, and calls it "the westernmost and best river," and its shores full of "goodly groves and woods." He found mast-pines and oaks in abundance, but not the sassafras, which was the patent medicine of the age, the very tree of life. With a store of sassafras one might live long and well, even in old England. Spain sought, in the same spirit, for the fountain of youth; and all nations for the transmutation of gold. It is curious to note how the early explorers found in America almost everything but the particular object of their adventure. There is one notable exception: some of them sought freedom and found it. New Hampshire forests were supposed to be full of the spicy sassafras; but they actually found mast-pine trees, which for many a year were a precious possession to England; and soon the broad arrow was seen everywhere, to the constant vexation and embroilment of the early settlers. In effect it was just like the game laws in their old home. Most of the mast timber and the oak were transported to the shipyards of England; although one fifty-four-gun ship, the Faulkland, was built at Portsmouth in 1690. Martin Pring saw no Indians; but Champlain, who touched here in 1605, found a party of them, who drew for him as much of the adjacent coasts as they knew. Champlain is supposed to have landed at what is now Odiorne's Point, on the south-western side of Little Harbor.

It is on Odiorne's Point that we hear at New Castle the rote of the sea, the premonition of storm. It is a melancholy sound, occurring at intervals of a minute, usually accompanying the retrogression of the third wave, which we always count the longest and largest. On a pebbly beach it draws back the small stones over each other, and as they rattle down there is produced that peculiar sound, which, heard at a distance, we call the rote. We anticipate wind and storm from that quarter; we must then look well to our moorings, and the householder must close the storm-door, which perhaps has been fastened back for a month.

After Champlain, came, in 1614, Capt. John Smith. He describes the situation here in a few words: "a safe harbor with a rocky shore." He gave their first name to the Isles of Shoals, after his own, Smith's Isles; and he also has the credit of christening New England. George Wither, the old English religious poet, in a poem addressed to him, has a line that corroborates the assertion:

"In that rude garden you New England stile."

The ancient navigators found these shores rude in the sense that the art of man had not been exercised upon them. The natural features, the virgin wealth, they saw and praised. They suspected great mineral resources, and for years the promoters of the first expeditions to the New Hampshire lands were constantly imploring the settlers "to find some good mines." They gratified them by sending to England specimens of the "Granite State!" We know now what they must have been; but what they themselves thought they were is indicated by a little inventory of minerals with which a vessel called the "Pide-Cow" returned to some English port about 1634. "The 5th of August the iron stone taken in the shipp; there is of 3 soartes, on sort that the myne doth cast forth as the tree doth gum, * * * on of the other soartes we take to be very rich."

These stones were taken from the vicinity of Dover. But they did not satisfy the English merchants who had planted the colonies here; one of whom writes back that "the christall stones you sent are of little or no value, unless they were so great to make drinking cupps or some other workes, as pillars for faire lookinge glasses, or for garnishing rich cabinets. Good iron or lead oare I should like better of, if it could be found." Nothing could be found under ground of any value; but the Great Carbuncle of the White Mountains and the fabulous scarlet muscle of Little Harbor remained to excite the imagination of the adventurers. Why these shores should have been thought by them to be a favorable location for vineyards seems strange; yet it must be remembered that the earlier explorers generally touched here in late spring or summer, when the verdure was wonderfully luxuriant and green, and their reports portrayed the country with a tropical pen; and in conversation, no doubt, with a still more exaggerated touch. The vine has not been a success. John Barleycorn has outdone the grape. Yet the ancient cellars were not without some choice wine for a wedding, and old rum for funerals was never wanting.

Meanwhile, the actual resources of the region, peltry, fishing and lumbering, continued to grow in importance, and became the foundations of substantial and prolonged prosperity. The pine conquered the sassafras, and silver was found more common in the mouth of the codfish, at the end of a hook, than at the point of a pick. Beyond all, as our Farmer's Almanac reminds us year after year, New Hampshire's choicest crop is men and women.

When the first settlement was made in New Castle is unknown; but as early as 1650 it was already a place of considerable importance. Its proximity to Odiorne's Point, just across Little Harbor, where the first house in New Hampshire was built, in 1623, is sufficient ground to suppose that this island must have been occupied very soon after the landing of the first company of settlers.

To see how natural is this supposition, let us take the short excursion from New Castle to Odiorne's Point. From the Wentworth Hotel the site is in plain view; by water it is a mile distant; by land it is two miles of pleasant, winding road: first south along the right bank of Sagamore Creek, then east and northeast through woodland roads, until we cross Seavey's Creek and are again in front of the ocean. In a half mile more we are beside a large farm-house under old elms; this is the Odiorne homestead, which has been in the family since 1660.

I promised the reader a visit to one more graveyard; and here, just south of the house, it is. Four stone walls enclose a little field, into which have sunk the rude memorials of the first New Hampshire graves. No inscriptions reveal names or dates; even the "unlettered muse" made no record; the simple pioneers had only the security of the final register. A few trees grow among the graves; the foot of an ancient walnut, ten feet in circumference, nearly covers one of the gravestones. Deciduous trees, and especially the walnut, grow so very slowly on the seashore, that I judge this tree to be at least two hundred years old. Near this yard, a little south, was the block-house, their citadel of safety; and probably a little chapel, for it is known that among the effects of the colony were articles of religious use. These are their names in an inventory of 1635:

"1 great bible,
12 service books,
1 pewter fllaggon,
1 communion cup,
2 fine tablecloths,
2 napkins."

These were for the service of peace and righteousness. Perhaps the reader would like to know what were their weapons of war, some of which, no doubt, were contained in their block-house. For heavy artillery they possessed pieces with formidable names, at least, as "*sakers*," "*minions*," "*rabenets*" and "*4 murthers;*" besides about two hundred small arms and thirteen barrels of powder. Their "two drums, fifteen recorders and hautboys," were probably the first musical instruments brought into New England. These drums, recorders, and hautboys are set down in the inventory under the head of "arms and ammunition;" but for what purpose were the last two musical instruments? All we can say is, they show the colony was not Puritan. Perhaps they expected to dance round the May-Pole; and they were not without proper partners for the dance, for the English company which sent out the colony provided twenty-two women, some of whom must have been unmarried, as the factor of the company here, Ambrose Gibbens, writes home for more married people, because "maids they are soone gonne in this countrie." They had for the fishing business "6 great shallops," "5 fishing boats with sails," and "13 skiffs." They had, also, two hundred and sixty-five domestic animals of different kinds, "two by two" for increase. This matter turned out according to the intention, for the same Ambrose Gibbens says, in one of his quaint, sententious letters to his principal, "Capt. Neale appoynted me two of your goates to keepe at his departinge. I praise God they are 4." The kine multiplied most, however; and the breed is said to be still perpetuated in this region. The only book in the old inventory, besides the Bibles and service books, is one on farming or gardening, in Latin, or at least with a Latin title, "*Georgius agricolæ.*" There are no remains of the block-house or other buildings near the burial-place, but the well is near by. A living spring in the bank of the beach, close to the settlement, is supposed to have been one of the chief conveniences that attracted the adventurers. Mason Hall, their principal building, and named for the grantee of the whole country now called New Hampshire, was situated on a slight eminence opposite the present Odiorne homestead. There is no record of the dimensions of this building. The name, Mason Hall, has a lofty, manorial sound; but I fear it would shrink to a rude and rather squalid structure were we able to reconstruct it of its original proportions and materials. Albeit, let the name and the sound remain to revive the imagination, by whose light we can most profitably explore the obscure beginnings of great enterprises. Whatever the building, the situation is noble. It is a slightly elevated and level promontory, sloping to the water, and including the land from Seavey's Creek to the mouth of Little Harbor. Nothing could show more discretion or finer perception of natural beauty than the site selected by our ancestors for the foundation of their enterprise. A friend of mine has said that the choice would have raised the reputation of a Phœnician navigator. He was nearly right. The best harbor on the coast; the mouth of a deep and broad river, easily defensible, and which they took care to fortify immediately; twenty islands between the sea and Portsmouth, green to the tide, where they meet the clearest of

waters; a climate tempered from excessive heat or cold by the ocean; with less fog, rain and east wind than is usual in seaside situations; surrounded by a fertile and well-timbered country,— certainly leave nothing to seek for loveliness and conveniency of habitation. There is no monument to mark the site of Mason Hall. Some part of its foundations may be traced; and you will be shown, on asking at the Odiorne homestead, an old raisin-box partly filled with the broken relics found about it; these consist of some iron and pewter utensils, broken pipes, bullets and moulds, and a three-pound cannon-ball, intended, doubtless, for a "saker" or "murther." Some portions of a human skeleton came to light in digging near the site of Mason Hall a few years since; these were laid upon the beam of an out- building and forgotten. At length the building was removed to another part of the grounds; the poor bones fell from their ignoble shelf, and when thought of again, could not be found.

So fares it with the Plymouth Rock of New Hampshire. The graves of its heroes neglected, their very bones lying about like broken crockery, and the relics of Mason Hall consigned to a raisin box! Shame upon the State of New Hampshire! What has she ever done to preserve her early history? Nothing but print a mass of confused and imperfect Provincial Papers. What does she know of Capt. Walter Neale, the first Governor of Little Har- bor settlement; he who discovered the White Mountains and made an expedition against Dixy Bull, the pirate of this coast? Is his portrait among the distinguished factory and railroad governors with which our State Capitol is adorning itself of late? We fear not; and still we believe he will pass down in history sometime after these other portraits will have become master-pieces of a lost art of perpetuating the obscure.

I must, then, before we leave Mason Hall, draw a small likeness of the man, in profile as it were, so that we may realize at least the characteristic outlines of the class of men who planted the first civilization here. They had few principles in common with the plantations at Plymouth and Massachusetts Bay. They had no ordinances against dancing, May Pole, falling bands or long hair; nor did they invent a hundred other petty, sumptuary devices to make this life as bleak as possible, and the next not worth having at current Puritan prices. At first they were royalists and churchmen; they changed at length and became like their neighbors, partly from force, partly from policy. But for some time there was much religious toleration in the New Hampshire settlement.

Massachusetts packed her Quakers off to Rhode Island; her Antinomians to New Hampshire. From 1650 to 1700 there were some very strange clergymen in Hampton, Portsmouth, and Dover. Their common weakness was Solomon's. One Rev. Thomas Larkham, of Dover, is on record as having had a damaging affair with a certain "handsome widow." The following epigram is feigned to be his own rather bold confession:

> I helped the Town, the Church re-edified,
>   And preached the people doctrine old and sound;
> I showed them how to ear the country-side,
>   And led the way on Widow Nutter's ground.

The civil officers, the agents, factors, sheriffs and governors were also a gay, fortune-hunting, philandering company, of whom Capt. Walter Neale was a conspicuous type; and I have promised his portrait to accompany Mason Hall, and which having glanced at, we will cross the water to Great Island, the original designation of New Castle.

Capt. Walter Neale was a true soldier of fortune; always ready for an expedition or campaign; always seeking that kind of employment from the English court or any transient patron among the gentry; always begging for something, and not averse to recounting his own services, merits and distresses. He describes himself, when seeking an appointment in these parts, as never having had any other profession but his sword, nor other fortunes than the war; and he adds pathetically that his debts are clamorous and his wants insupportable. When not otherwise engaged he acted as captain and drill-master of the London militia. He was a free lance, among the last of the knights-errant, and of the Round Table. Such was the first governor of New Hampshire and all the lands to the eastward of Massachusetts Bay. He has nothing in common with the solemn and pragmatical Winthrops and Endicotts; and instead of settling quietly down at Mason Hall to found a church and raise corn, he goes in search of the fabled land of Laconia, in expectation of finding precious stones and mines of gold. Arriving at the White Mountains and picking up what resembled crystals, he named them the Crystal Hills. For three years he explored the woods, planned fortifications, drilled the settlers in arms, and chased pirates. He is a typical character, of the same family of Raleigh, Smith, and Standish; men who discovered new countries, founded colonies, — uniting the real and the romantic as never before, — and went trading and exploring round the world, writing love songs and marvellous narratives, and all as if it were the pastime of the moment, and every day would bring a "noble chance."

As we stand on the site of Mason Hall, New Castle is in full view and looks inviting. So it must have appeared to the first settlers, and being so near they soon took possession of it. Sometime between 1623 and 1635, must be the date of its first occupation, for by the recent transcript of a document in the English archives, it appears that between those years, the company sent out by John Mason to occupy his grant, had not only founded the Mason Hall and its defences, but "did build many houses upon the *great Island*, which lyeth at the entrance of said river (Pascattaway) upon which he [the proprietor here puts himself for his agents] erected a ffort and mounted it with tenn Guns for the Defence of said Island and River."

The ground for the fort was laid out on the northeast point of the island, and was meant to extend from the water to the high ledge, on which now stands Walbach's Martello Tower. This place has always been known as Fort Point, and has been alternately fortified and neglected since the earliest times. It was called The Castle, in the early time, then Fort William and Mary, and during the Revolution, Fort Hancock; and when it was rebuilt in 1808, probably received its present name, Fort Constitution. Since the close of the Rebellion, Fort Constitution has been nothing but a melancholy ruin; parts of the old walls are standing, and the new are left unfinished. Never could you see anywhere such a waste of buildings, building materials, tools, and property of every sort, by sheer neglect, as at Fort Constitution during the last fifteen years. It has not even a flag-staff; and we should never know in New Castle when it was the 22d of February or July 4th, but for the bonfire and excellent drum-corps of our patriotic boys. Its garrison consists of a single soldier, an ordnance-serjeant. In the earliest times it was manned entirely by citizens of New Castle, who, in consequence, were exempted from other military duties, in campaigns against the Indians and French. At length they grew weary of the "constant burden of watching and warding," petitioned to be relieved, and men were drawn from other places for the purpose. The first commanding officer of the Fort was Richard Cutts, in 1674, whose lieutenant was Elias Stileman; both were New Castle men. On the death of Cutts, Stileman became captain, and continued in the office a long time. The old Fort, though several times alarmed, has never fired a belligerent gun. It has been once captured, but not by an enemy, and without bloodshed. The event antedates Lexington and Concord by nearly four months; and it is passing strange that so significant a circumstance should be almost unknown and unnoticed.

New Castle was the scene of the first important aggressive armed action of the Revolutionary patriots.

The story is one of the interesting episodes that open the history of the Revolution, and was the first overt act of the rebellion against the military power of England; the first of which the English government received official notice. It is associated, too, with one of the romantic figures of the times, Paul Revere. Before Paul Revere's ride to Lexington and Concord, he had taken a much longer one, if not as celebrated. On the 13th of December, 1774, he rode express from Boston to Portsmouth, dispatched by the Boston Committee of Safety, to inform the similar organization in Portsmouth of the new order of the British, that no gunpowder or military stores should be exported to America. No doubt this information was coupled with advice to secure the gunpowder at Fort William and Mary, before the arrival of a large garrison, reported also, by Paul Revere, to be on its way. Therefore, the next night, or next day (the 14th), the Portsmouth "Sons of Liberty," with the patriots of New Castle, in all about four hundred, under command of Maj. John Sullivan and Capt. John Langdon*— he who afterward offered his "hard money," plate, and "seventy hogsheads of Tobago rum" to the service of the State; first president of the United States Senate and governor of New Hampshire — proceeding to the fort by water, as there were then

---

* Some authorities say Capt. John Pickering also.

no bridges, invested it and summoned Capt. John Cochran and his five soldiers to surrender. However, it was not the officers and men, nor yet the fort they came for, but its one hundred barrels of powder, which they carried away and secreted under Durham meeting-house. The subsequent history of this powder is equally interesting with its capture; for most of it was used at Bunker Hill, being carted there by oxen all the way from Durham town, just in season to be served to the soldiers on the eve of the engagement; and the last ounce of it was fired in 1800, from the shotgun formerly belonging to Sir William Pepperell, and found as fatal to the Madbury gray squirrels as it had been to King George's red-coats.

Paul Revere's ride, the expedition and capture of the fort, the subsequent service of the powder in the first battle of the Revolution, and its final peaceful report in the Madbury woods, taken together do make a suggestive and poetic story. There is also a comic aspect in poor Capt. Cochran and his five soldiers (two of them being recruited for this occasion) at the mercy of four hundred men; and the humorous is furnished by the countersign of the Sons of Liberty while preparing the attack:

> "We are going to take a glass of wine
> With Captain Cockerine, Cockerine."*

Nor is this all the history; there is much more incident, too much for this place. Suffice it to say, that this same powder effectually blew up the royal administration of Gov. John Wentworth at Portsmouth and throughout the Province of New Hampshire; so that he had to report to his superiors in the same language of his predecessor, Capt. Walter Neale, concerning the

---

* There are many MS. letters of Cochran in the New Hampshire archives. We give the signature of one of them.

Laconian Utopia—"*non est inventa provincia.*" The last scenes in the official career of Gov. Wentworth take us to New Castle; and his star finally sets at the Isles of Shoals. In fear of his life, he fled to Fort William and Mary, now for a brief period under the protection of the British men-of-war, the Scarborough and Canceaux, from whence he attempted to exercise his office, in vain. Soon he sails for Boston; and not long after ventures to return, but no nearer than the Isles of Shoals, where, on September 24th, 1775, he issues his last proclamation to the rebels of New Hampshire.

It was while the British ships, just alluded to, were at anchor in the harbor and were supposed to be about to destroy New Castle and Portsmouth, that the fascinating Mary Sparhawk, the Tory belle of Kittery, captivated the heart of the Canceaux' commander, Capt. Mowatt, and changed his fell purpose. She thought Portland would do just as well to sack as Portsmouth; and so he sailed away to that port and burned four hundred houses.

Fort William and Mary seems to have been abandoned during the Revolution; and new defences were erected on the islands nearer Portsmouth. These earthworks are still visible, and on their southern slopes the grass, in spring, is earlier green than elsewhere along the Piscataqua. A deep peace has settled over them; nature has smoothed and rounded all traces of their hostile purpose; there the cattle now pasture, or climb the parapets in summer afternoons to ruminate, and face the cool breeze from the outer sea. And I must not forget the serjeant's cow at Fort Constitution, which wanders and feeds over the ruined enclosure, cropping the sweet herbage, which so soon endeavors to obliterate and beautify the negligence and devastation of man.

At the southeast angle of Fort Constitution is Fort Point lighthouse, the inner light of Portsmouth harbor. The first structure was built under the administration of Gov. John Wentworth in 1771. Previous to that period, the only light shown was a lantern from the flagstaff of the fort. Gov. Wentworth appealed to the Provincial Assembly for a grant sufficient for the lantern; and later, for the lighthouse. He told the Assembly in his best rhetoric, that "Every future expiring cry of a drowning Mariner upon our coast, will bitterly accuse the unfeeling Recusant that wastes that Life to save a paltry unblessed Shil-

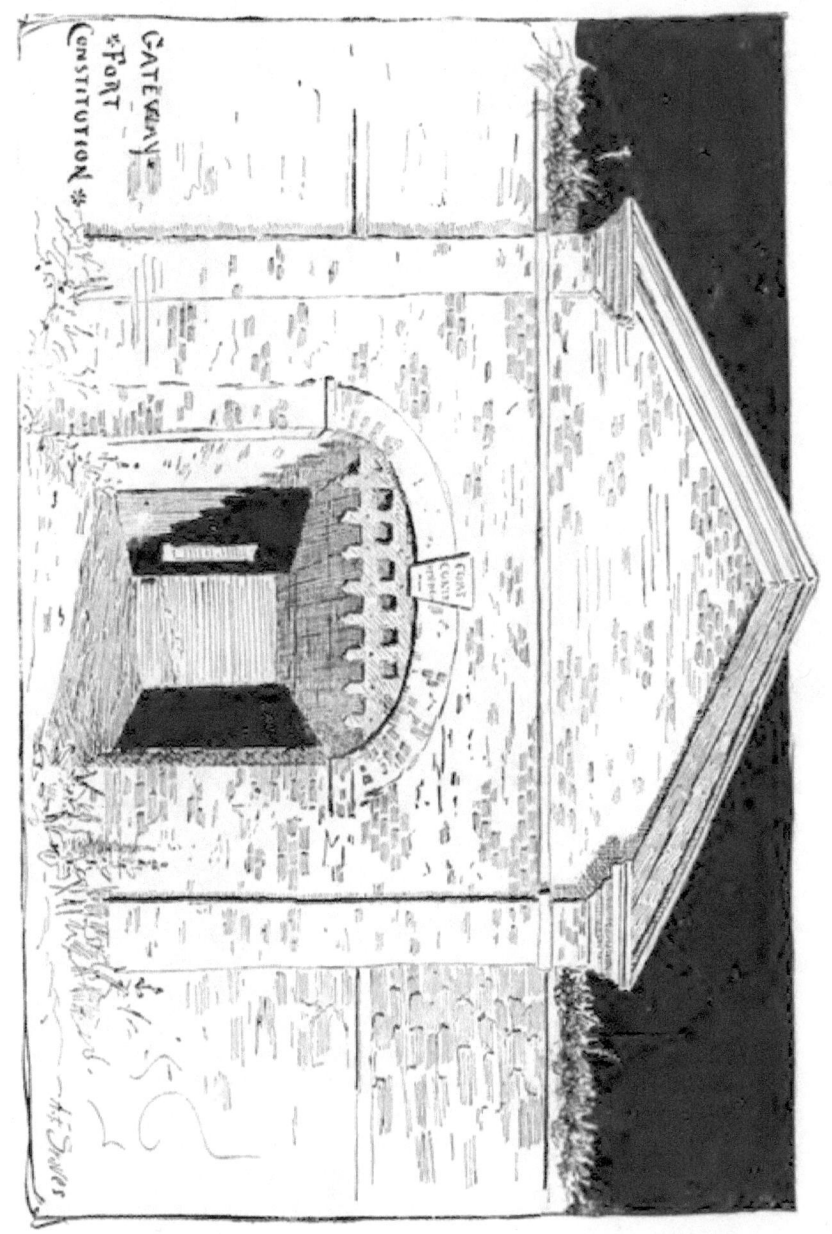

ling." But shillings, blessed or unblessed, were scarce in those days; and the Assembly talked of squandering the people's money, after the current manner. However, the Governor built the lighthouse, and left the Assembly to pay for it afterwards. It was of wood, and plenty of it. If shillings were not abundant, timber was; and there was more than enough in the old structure to build a modern house. It was eight-sided, and straddled the rocks like a wooden Colossus. The main timbers were ninety feet in height and eighteen inches square, and must have been of primeval growth. The base diameter of the building was forty feet. It was built to endure, and a thousand years would have been a moderate limit to its usefulness. In 1789 it was ceded by the State to the United States. In 1854 it was shortened to sixty feet, so as not to be mistaken for Whalesback, the outer harbor light. In 1879 it was pulled down, and a hideous iron tower took its place, which resembles nothing so much as a length of corpulent stove-pipe, set on end — and painted.

The Martello Tower, a little west of the Fort and the lighthouse, is the most picturesque object in New Castle. It is built on the ridge of a high ledge, anciently called Jourdan's Rocks. Artists have painted it, and poets love to relate its story, relying upon each other for imaginary embellishments. Its date is so recent and its history so small, that it is almost necessary to invent some facts, in order properly to celebrate so rare a ruin. One feels that if it has not a legend it ought to have.

THE LEGEND OF WALBACH TOWER.

(NEW CASTLE N. H. A. D. 1814.)

If you should turn your feet from yonder town
Intent to bathe your eyes with healing sight
Of open sea, and islands rising through,
Mere heaps of shattered ledge that have outstood
Eternal storm, though gray, defiant still,
The river shows the path that you must go;
Its stream engralls the shores of twenty isles,

And pleasant is the way as is its end;
For you will idle on the bridges three,
And loiter through the ancient village street,
That crowns the harbor mouth; then you will come
To beaches hard, and smoothed by each new tide
Rolling between the low, port-cullised rocks,
Rocks bare a-top, but kirtled at the feet
With sea-weed draperies that float or fall,
As swells or sinks the lonely, restless wave.
There, just above the shore, is Walbach Tower,
Its crumbling parapet with grass and weeds
O'ergrown, and peaceful in its slow decay.
Old people always tell strange tales to us,
A later race — always old tales are strange.
And seems the story of this ancient Tower
A marvel, though believing while I hear,
Because who tell it do believe it true.
Three English ships lay under Appledore,
And men in groups stood on the rocks, intent
If they the fort could mean to cannonade,
Or land along the coast and inland march
To sack and burn the wealthy Portsmouth Town.
The morning dawned and twice again it dawned,
And still the hostile ships at anchor swung;
But now a rumor ran they meant to land;
At once brave Walbach was resolved to build
A tower which all the beaches should command,
And mount thereon his sole tremendous gun.
He summoned all the villagers at dusk
Of one September Sunday when the days
Are shortening, and the nights are bright and cool.
Men came and boys, and with them women came,
Whose dauntless mothers helped our fathers win,
In that rebellious time against the king,
The freedom which, forgetful of its cost,
We toss to any hand raised o'er the crowd,
And pushing hardest, or with loudest voice.
They wrought as never men and women wrought,
And in one night the Tower completed rose.

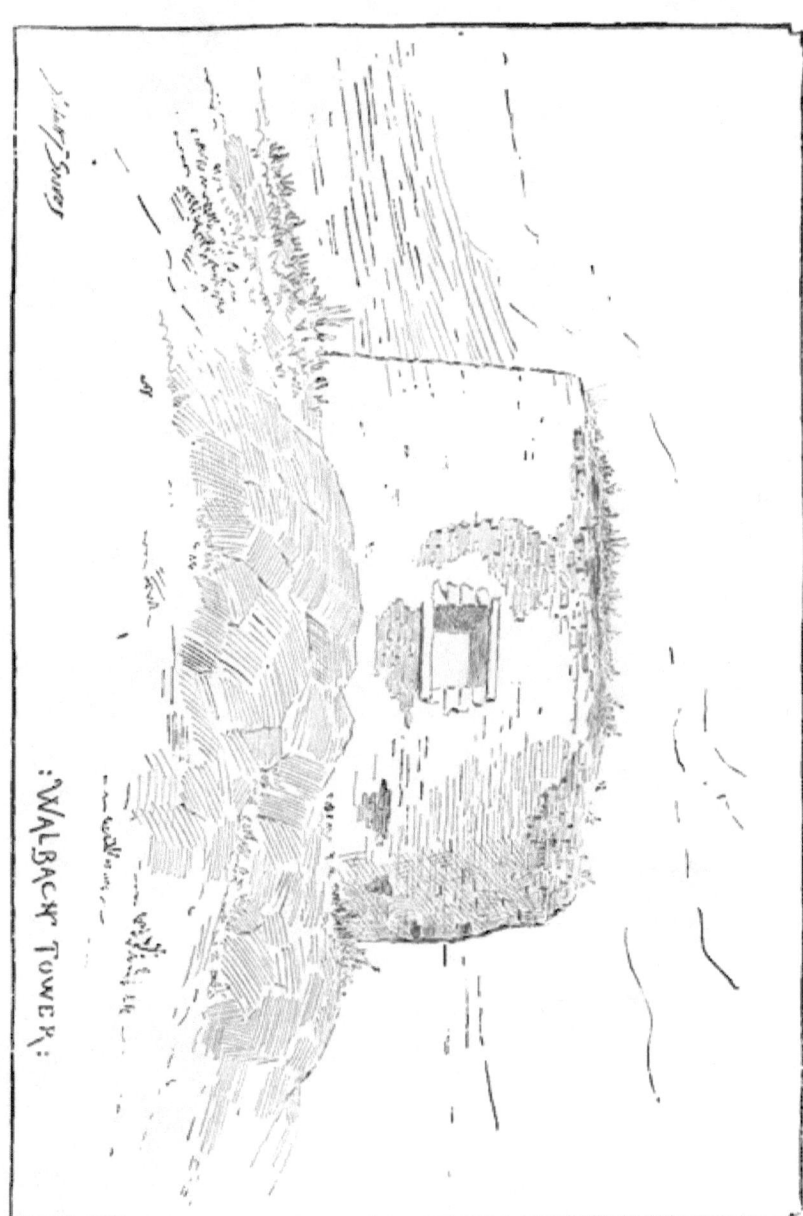

But lo, the miracle! for unseen hands
Alternate with the mason's dextrous craft,
As voice repeats and catches up the voice
In song, laid on the workmen's every course
Another course, and they no presence saw,
But thought they heard the chiming trowels ring.
The morning glimmer showed that labor done
For which two nights were counted scarce enough;
Then well their awed but joyful hearts confessed
Some present deity their champion friend,
To whom they knelt upon the dewy grass,
As in the east, the sun returning, built
A tower of gold along the ocean floor,
And offered up subdued and grateful praise.
The hateful ships approached the river mouth,
Stood off and on and tacked about; at last,
Firing a gun to stern, they sailed away.

Still stands the Tower, long may it stand, disused!
Without a blow, one foe it put to flight;
And when another comes it will arise
And in its ruins keep its legend good.
For while I told this tale one summer night,
Leaning a weary head on fondest breast,
We heard the sea-maids on the outer rocks
Splash in the falling tide, and dimly saw
What seemed their tresses, undulating there;
And felt, around, below, above, the power,
Not human, but the help of human hands,
When set to labor in some noble cause.

The annals say that the Tower was built during the last war with England, and when an immediate attack was expected by an English fleet. Its purpose was to guard more effectually the so-called Town Beach, to the south, from landing parties: and to reinforce the batteries of Fort Constitution. It was planned and constructed under the care of Col. Walbach, whose name it has always borne. He was a German Count, who had seen service in the Prussian army and fought against Napoleon in twenty-six battles. He was long in the service of the United States, and in command of Fort Constitution from 1806 to 1821. Col. Walbach summoned the company of sixty men, under Capt. Marshall, who garrisoned the earthworks on Jaffrey's Point, at the eastern end of New Castle, to assist his own soldiers in building the Tower; and all the citizens of the town also aided. It was rapidly completed; but no enemy appeared, and soon the Tower grew a ruin. It is so small as to suggest a fortification in miniature or model, rather than for actual use. It is of the size of the round towers of the Middle Ages; and on this account, perhaps, appears of greater antiquity — of the age the imagination easily renders it. Indeed, it seems incredible that seventy years should have wrought so complete and perfect a resemblance to ruined castles and towers long antedating this. But these are fast ages; time itself has caught the trick of counterfeiting the mark of its former slowness, and antiquates our constructions in half its former periods. Walbach Tower is of brick; the terreplein was of peat, which has become like grassy turf. I have burned some of it in the evening fire, and found its smoke still fragrant. It was cut from Col. Walbach's own swamp, adjacent to Jaffrey Cottage, which he then occupied, and was intended for his winter fuel. After seventy years, it is pleasant to see its glow in the fireplace of its first intention. The Tower is difficult of access now, as the entrance is partially obstructed by fallen bricks and mortar. It never was high enough to walk through; and now you must enter on all-fours. Within is a rude pintle-stone, on which to swing a thirty-two-pounder. There are three casemated embrasures for small cannon or muskets, in case of assault; and a Liliputian magazine. The United States military engineers had threatened to destroy this venerable and quaint relic at the time when they were constructing the new walls of Fort Constitution, in 1863–65; but their intention was frustrated by their own work being found ineffectual, and only fit to be abandoned to that decay which is the fashion of all government property in this neighborhood. However, the vandal spirit found its opportunity on Jaffrey's Point, in 1874, when the earthworks there were begun. On this Point were probably the oldest defences along the coast. They were of the most primitive construction; six low, semi-circular parapets in front of a heavy

: Boatswain Allens House :

stone-wall, flanked on the right by a long gully between two ledges, on which were two other, and perhaps more, parapets. Inside was a deep well of good water. They were on the northeasterly side of the promontory, and quite close to the water. I believe that here is where were planted the six brass pieces given to the colonists by the merchants of London, and that this site was fortified earlier than that of the present Fort Constitution; I believe it to have been under the direction of Capt. Walter Neale. I endeavored to save these ancient memorials of the forefathers of New Hampshire, in vain. Then I requested the engineers to make an accurate drawing of their position and form, so to preserve at least the record and evidence of their former existence; but they did not listen; and this page, and the accompanying drawing, which I have made from memory, but which may be trusted, must be the only testimony concerning them. They were wantonly and needlessly destroyed, for

First Fort at the mouth of the Piscataqua

they were neither in the way of the new works, nor did they furnish much available material for them; and in the end have only been a contribution toward what has been abandoned to become itself a ruin.

There were other more recent earthworks on Jaffrey Point which were also thrown into the new; so that here, as at Fort Constitution, ruins overlay ruins, of three or four periods. Some were built in 1812-14. and were garrisoned by sixty yeomanry militia under Capt. Marshall, of whom mention has been made in connection with Walbach Tower. He was accustomed to drill his men in the parlor of the Jaffrey Cottage, which is directly behind Jaffrey Point, and they used the homestead barn for barracks. The same Jaffrey parlor was used also as the meeting place of the Provincial Assembly in 1682-83, when Cranfield was Lieutenant-Governor of New Hampshire. This parlor (or hall, as sometimes called) forms a large and incongruous portion of the cottage, and was used for various public purposes in former times, not the least curious of which were "small-pox parties," in days when people retired from the world to be inoculated. It was not very serious business, and young folks made a holiday of it, and were said to do considerable courting on such occasions. I fancy some names scratched on the window-panes of the Jaffrey parlor, still visible, are mementos of that time of tenderness, and — sore arms. The cottage has always been a favorite resort of lovers, than whom there are no human beings more easy or pleasant to entertain. Satisfied with themselves and each other, you share in the benevolence of the rosy illusion, and your hospitality seeks to be unrestricted. At such times, the small, sea-moated farm flows with milk and honey and never too much; for I find, contrary to common observation, that lovers have, whether from the saline situation or in compliment to the unworthy host, the most extraordinary appetites. The sequel of these little histories has often been celebrated in the great parlor in numberless marriages. Of course, also, in seven generations of dwellers, the feet of them that carry out the dead have often been heard at the door. It lends a kind of sanctity to the old house to think how many souls have lived and died here; how many strangers, too, now dust, have looked out of its windows. Once Longfellow peered pensively out of them upon the sea, musing his Lady Wentworth ballad; once Mrs. Stowe stooped through the attic to wonder at the huge beams and chimney-pile; and many other poets and romancers have passed in and out the house, adding modern memories to its ancient archive. And now, on the adjoining shore, a poet has come to abide, and enrich this seat of olden, local renown, with his wide and living fame.

Jaffrey Point has the Piscataqua on the left and Little Harbor on the right, and in front the open sea, unbroken save where the Isles of Shoals, six miles off, show their low outline. Often, however, the mirage elevates them, and then they resemble the

chalk cliffs of the English Channel; sometimes changing to the battlements and towers of a feudal city, then fading away, as if raised and dispelled by enchantment. Every day brings some variation in their appearance. Though anchored, they seem to have the mobility of the sky and the water. One day they are on the farthest horizon line; another, they are but a step, and you can almost hear their sweet syren singing her song as she tends her flowers, or paints them on the leaves of her book.

It is the south wind which here brings with it the mirage, and transforms the islands and shores into fairyland; the mirage is nature's imagination.

It was an Indian tradition that heaven was in the southwest, and that the world was made with the wind in that quarter, which one can well believe on summer days of soft haze and mirage; for then it seems as if nature were playing and experimenting with myriad forms, any one of which she could make permanent as easily as the one we know. But the Isles of Shoals have other aspects less fanciful, and more useful to us who dwell near to them on the mainland. They are our weather-glass; and we judge of the day or the morrow, whether to fish or to plant, according to their monitions. To forecast the weather we need a wide and distant horizon; and if there be some intervening object, like an island, it seems to catch and concentrate the far-off signals of change, announcing the coming storm or fair day or shifting wind. The Isles of Shoals, the pimpernel, the movements of the sea-birds, the rote on Odiorne's Point, or, if your bones are old or have been broken, your rheumatism, these prognosticators make us wondrous weather-wise at New Castle.

The southern side of New Castle, from Jaffrey's Point to Leach's Island, is bounded by Little Harbor. Formerly, New Castle included also the territory on the other side of Little Harbor, which now forms a part of the town of Rye.

The south part of New Castle was occupied first, being next to and very near the earliest settlement, on Odiorne's Point. There seem to have been two movements from Mason Hall; one toward the west, along the "Strawberry Patch Road," (which I shall hereafter describe) the seat of the Sherburnes, Slopers, Lears and Langdons; and the other north, across New Castle, up the right bank of the Piscataqua and upon both shores of Little Harbor. For the last half century, however, there have been only two or three private dwellings upon this, the southern portion of New Castle. But cellar-holes are almost as numerous as the graves, to which I have previously alluded. Some have been filled, others overgrown; yet an apple-tree or wild-cherry, or some half wild garden-flower usually marks the site. A surer token is a plot of very black earth, which, when turned by the plough, discovers broken clam-shells, bits of earthenware; and when cultivated, the mallow, thistle and burdock are sure to spring up. Here, we thus may know, was the back-yard or kitchen entrance, over which the wastage of some house spread itself. As there are man-loving birds and animals, so certain weeds and plants love the country house-yards; and are kindly to men; for, being generally large-leaved and rank growers, they absorb the noxious matter thrown from the house.

Here, we may be sure, were no large or commodious dwellings. They were small and low, unplastered, with two doors only, and few windows or none. The chimney and fireplace were the most important feature; and the good-wives cooked by the same fire that warmed the family. If they went to bed warm they were sure to get up in the cold. But not so the fireplace, where, buried in ashes, slumbered the brands and the coals, to be raked open in the early morning and make everybody soon comfortable, and to furnish forth the warm breakfast of corn-meal, fish, wild game, or pork. I presume that Jaffrey Cottage, humble as it now seems, was in its day — the last half of the seventeenth century — a house of the larger and more pretentious sort. It had the rare distinction of three fires; one for cooking, one to sit by, and a third to warm your night-gown at. It alone survives of all the dwellings of the period, in the south part of New Castle. But history repeats itself in little as in large; and again the modern world has found its way into New Castle on that side, over the new free bridge of Little Harbor. drawn by the fine situation of the Wentworth Hotel, and the advantages for private summer residences along the shore.

The free bridge over Little Harbor was built in 1875, by the towns of New Castle and Rye, aided by an appropriation of $1400 from the County of Rockingham. Its length is 730 feet, and its total cost something over $7,000. It is the successor of one built by a stock company in the beginning of this century, and which,

on account of want of travel and bad management, was suffered to go to decay; and at length its owners took away, each one, such a portion as they thought themselves entitled to. A curious fate for a bridge. I have heard that the toll-collector sold rum to eke out his living, and that, at the last, he was obliged to take huckleberries in summer and clams in winter in payment of toll. Besides, every one was allowed to pass free on Sunday, as passengers were presumed to be going to meeting. When the new bridge was built hardly a trace of the former one could be seen; but the new is exactly on the line of the old. The old name of the place where the bridge lands in Rye was Saunders' Point. In the beginning of the seventeenth century there was a ferry at the same point, supported at the charge of New Castle; and a little later there was probably a rude bridge across the narrowest part of Little Harbor, from Blunt's Island to the beach, near the house of Mr. Charles Campbell. On the site of Mr. Campbell's house was one of the earliest dwellings in New Castle. It was near and on the natural path to the ancient tide-mill, where our little local history has been again repeated by re-building a dam over the old one, in order to confine the tide-water as a pleasure lake for the children guests of the Wentworth Hotel.

At certain seasons of the year, the Indians were in the habit of camping on the New Castle side of Little Harbor, at a place once called Manwarring's Orchard, and feasting on clams and muscles. On the bluff, southeast from Wentworth Hotel, their shell-mounds may be observed. I presume on opening them Indian relics might be found, but I have never attempted it; I like to see them as they are, their little mystery unexplored, their secrets their own.

Antiquities are precious in their proper tombs, not in the closets of predaceous museums. I like the Ilium of Homer better than that of Dr. Schlieman. So, if any traveller should chance upon our shell-mounds, let him know they are pre-empted — an Indian reservation.

Walking from the Wentworth Hotel toward the village of New Castle you pass on the right, near the lane leading to Jaffrey Point, the glebe land apportioned in old times to the use of the parson of the town. In one corner of it was a Potter's Field, now overgrown with pines.

Many original local designations linger in New Castle, the most curious of which are the names still given to the south and north parts of the island. The south part is known as *Oatalong*, and the north as *Inalong*. I find both of these names in the town records.

From whatever direction one approaches the village portion of New Castle — the *Inalong* of the natives — he is struck by its compactness. It is built upon the right bank of the Piscataqua. Two irregular streets follow the general direction of the river, and run through nearly the extent of the populous portion of the village. A few cross streets start from the upper of the two just named and end at the water side, or continue as a pathway to some outlying dwelling. An island town, and for several generations without bridges to the mainland, horses and carriages were unknown, and consequently the streets have all the characteristics that are common where they have grown out of lanes and pathways, convenient foot passages from one house to another. The cows cannot be held responsible for them here, but the situation of the houses, which, having been placed according to accident or necessity, are now left at various angles with the straightened or widened streets.* The dwellings have a decided individuality, and are the growth of time and many minds. Little of the antique remains to them, however, save their venerable frameworks. They have been moved and remodelled; a story has been razed or added, and new doors and modern windows now conceal the primitive construction. The ingenious modern mind invented white paint and the green blind, and they were adopted here, though late. Those who did not follow the custom now find themselves in fashion; and the oldest and newest houses in New Castle alike show the natural colors of pine and cedar and seem already coeval. There is no eminence from which one can observe so well the circular movement in certain matters of taste, as in an old town which has been invaded by the æsthetic architect and his wealthy patrons. As some children are said to be born old, so must the quite new house by skilful devices wear at once the look of antiquity, and have nothing recent but its occupants, who by some equal art appear to be forever young.

---

* From 1820 to 1830, there was a great rage for rectifying our old lanes and alleys; and I suspect that the town lost half its ancient features in that period.

Ere the days of ground lead, red ochre and whitewash were common substitutes; and some who affected gentility used a yellow wash for interior decoration. But in general, the interiors were wainscoted with pine, some specimens of which still remain, of noble width and without a knot, sheets of the great trees once marked by the "broad arrow" of England. I have measured one of twenty-eight inches, and have heard of one of thirty-six. When left unpainted they assume, in a century or two, a rich coffee color, and have a peculiarly agreeable smell, something like the forests in autumn. They may be said then to be ripe and fit to shelter the household divinities. Ruskin says a house is not fit to be lived in until three hundred years old.

After wainscoting came plastering; this was usually of lime mortar, though not always. There is found on the beaches of New Castle, covered by a foot of sand or gravel, a blue clay, which was used sometimes for plastering, and quite generally in laying the stone or brick chimneys. It is still used for stove-linings and any small repairs — "to stop a hole to keep the wind away." It is good also for cementing the joints of drain-tile. Indeed, our forefathers wanted not ample materials for building, yet this abundance did not so often suggest to them spacious structures, as the means of strength and solidity. The small habitation of George Jaffrey has timber like a ship, and a chimney twelve feet square at the base and four at top. And I have already mentioned the size of the main posts of the old Fort Point lighthouse. You may calculate on a year's supply of fuel when you make any change, tear down or build over any part of a New Castle house. An old house is therefore cheap at any price, even for fuel; and I begrudge the bargain of Mr. Joseph Simpson who, in 1704, bought one of our old meeting-houses for fifty shillings — "for ye frame and what boards was to it."

Modern improvements have obscured most of the ancient, external features of New Castle, which once made it so quaint. But the situation of the houses is generally the same; the streets follow the old lanes; and the shores, where the life of the village mostly centres, are unchanged. Portions of the Provincial Court and Council House are now dwelling-houses, one of which the illustration shows, with its low wall and sharp pitched roof.* New Castle was for a long period the seat of the Provincial government and residence of the governors.

The Province House stood on a slight eminence opposite the head of the road, leading from the village to Fort Constitution. The foundations are still visible, and its well yet in use. There are people now living who remember when a part of it was standing, and was known as the "Old Sloop." Here again I must remark that it is a reproach to the State of New Hampshire, to leave unhonored the sites of its most ancient public buildings. Not one of the New England States has done so little to preserve the memorials of its early history as ours. Is it true, as some poet said?

> "The God who made New Hampshire
> Taunted the lofty land
> With little men."

The Sheafe family was, in the seventeenth and eighteenth centuries, among the most important in business and public affairs in New Castle; and their ancestral house stood near the Province House, at the corner of the roads leading from the village to the Fort and Wentworth Hotel. We are unable to point out the family seats of the Atkinsons, the Stilemans, Eliots, Bells, Frosts, Lears. The Prescott house was on the river side, near the town wharf. The cellar yet remains. Though called the Prescott house, it was built by a member of the Pepperell family, and was occupied at various times by the Provincial governors. Its modern history is curious. It belonged for a time to the town and was used as a poor-house; this use having come to an end, it was converted into a tenement-house; next leased, on condition of certain repairs being made by the lessee, which condition was not satisfactorily complied with and brought a long law-suit upon the town. At length the town sold it, together with its very valuable wharf privilege, to a firm engaged in the fish business, for a merely nominal sum. This business being removed to Portsmouth, the property passed into the hands of the Prescotts again, descend-

---

*I have little doubt it was, in reality, a private house, the old Atkinson mansion, but given up for public purposes.

: Portion of old ·
: Province House :

ants of the original family. By them it was torn down. After several more transfers the land on which it stood, and all the other buildings and wharves attached to it, were last sold to Hon. Frank Jones. I remember the old house well; it was of two stories, spacious, with much fine wainscoting. The hall went through the building, and from it arose a noble staircase with double landings, a handsome baluster with curiously carved newel-posts, of two different patterns, alternately set. At the head of the first landing was a lofty, arched window, at the bottom of which was a deep seat, forming, when the window-draperies were half drawn, almost a boudoir. It would hold two persons, tête-à-tête; and here, I have heard an old lady say, she lost her heart.

The situation was as fine as the house, washed by the river, and surrounded by great trees. It was strange and sad, yet had a melancholy fitness, that the old manse should be finally pulled down by the family with whose name it had so long been associated. Time is not so ruthless as the passion for improvement, and —

"Down the old house goes!'

"On these oaken floors
  High-shoed ladies trod;
Through these panelled doors
  Trailed their furbelows;
Long their day has ceased;
  Now, beneath the sod,
With the worms they feast, —
  Down the old house goes!

Many a bride has stood
  In yon spacious room;
Here her hand was wooed
  Underneath the rose;
O'er that sill the dead
  Reached the family tomb:
All that were have fled, —
  Down the old house goes!"

As we walk on past the site of the Prescott house, we come in a few minutes to a queer hip-roofed house, perched on the very brink of the river, so near, in fact, that the back door is a boat-landing. This house was once the home of Commodore Paul Jones' boatswain, Allen. Its age is unknown, but can be traced one hundred and fifty years, and is supposed to be one of the oldest buildings in New Castle. Its interior is in no way remarkable, except for its chambers, about the size of an old-fashioned ship's cabin. The vegetable garden in front of the house has been always noticeable for its neatness and thriftiness, and for containing the same plants in the same places for a generation past. The next building to boatswain Allen's house is the post-office and village store. Here let us stop and listen to a yarn from Capt. John.

Capt. John is the story-teller of New Castle; an artist of the naive kind; a poet without verse. His instinct for effects, for small, piquant touches, is excellent. In all his stories he has been an eye-witness, and generally a participant. His tales are always dramatic; there are actors with clear individuality, and he reports their speech in their own words, makes them actual in his scenes by a natural objective sense, so that you recognize them all through his narratives. He has a whole shelf full of stories, more moving and extraordinary than any on mine. One listens, believes too, and never tires. We who hear them have the same experience as children: we can hear them again and again; and Capt. John has no reluctance, he has told them to more than one generation; he knows their power and that he can hold his audience as well at the twentieth as at the first recital. Though nearly four-score, his memory is wonderful — memory, mother of all the muses, however humble; and imagination, the vivid touch which makes you see what he sees, must have been his birthright. Ah, I often think what a writer of plays or of fiction was lost in him! Hearing him, I understand how our old English adventurers not only could see, perform and suffer so much, but also had a natural gift for narration.

Capt. John has been a deep-water sailor all his life; has sailed in every kind of vessel and wherever water flows. He has been on whaling voyages and trading voyages; tempests, wrecks, pirates, pestilence, starvation and thirst, prodigies in the heavens and in the seas, adventures and perils in strange ports, hair-

Here she lost Her heart

breadth 'scapes, he knows, and has experienced all that a sailor can and live.

The moving accident has been his trade and is now his theme. He has softer pages, however, in his entertaining volumes: balmy, entrancing scenes in southern latitudes, where he barely escaped beautiful syrens with dark eyes, and cheeks blushing through the brown; rich in doubloons and lands; all, all should be his, would he but stay! And often now the old man regrets his hard heart and wishes he had yielded. But in those old days his island home was dearer to him than all the world beside, though he saw it but rarely, and then only to refit and sail again. His stories are of various lengths, but in a certain sense they all have a connection; the shorter are merely episodes, portions of longer ones which belong in the history of a year or a round voyage. Of a winter's day, in the village store, he sometimes begins in the morning, adjourns for dinner, continues through the afternoon, adjourns for supper, and concludes in the evening, one narrative all the day long. He is the last of the village skippers who sailed beyond the Banks and the West Indies. His is no coast-wise experience.

It would be natural to suppose that a man of such observation and memory for distant transactions, would know all that had happened at home, and he has indeed a store of local memories. He recalls past generations of men and women, their manners and the remarkable incidents in their lives; how they used to smuggle rum and coffee, their quarrels, their jests and songs, their extempore rhymes, their house-raisings, their dress, opinions, superstitions and peccadilloes. He tells of the ship captain who, going on a voyage, orders a house of three stories, but returning with bad luck, shortened it to two; and, after another unsuccessful venture, finishes it in one story.

Thus Capt. John enlivens the past with quaint and graphic details. Others may tell the fact, he knows all the circumstances. His memory is not only longer than that of others, but of a different order; it is like a tree full of foliage compared with the stark and winter bough of common memory. Capt. John is but one, and almost the last, of a class of men once living here who must have made life extremely agreeable and picturesque; who, in fact, supplied some of the elements of education, and the lack of books and newspapers. Although isolated when at home, they had the whole world in their mind and memory, and knew as well as Gœthe, it was made so wide that they might wander and learn.

I should but spoil one of Capt. John's narratives in repeating; so I will ask the reader to walk on a little farther, past a plot of green grass about as large as a table-cloth, where three ways meet; to which a certain little girl, if she were with us, would be sure to call our attention and repeat her joke about the "village green." Keeping on, we come where the road branches into two, which again unite at a half mile, taking us to Portsmouth. All roads lead to Portsmouth from an insular necessity. Following the lower or shore road, we pass the last of the Lombardy poplars now left in New Castle, and wind around a cove which was once the scene of great activity in the days when the fishing business was the chief interest. Here, at these decaying piers, in early spring, the small vessels fitted out for a cruise to the Banks and eastern shores; and returning in fall, spread their fares on the flakes which covered all the adjacent fields. In winter, the vessels were mostly laid up; a few went on trading voyages to the West Indies, taking dried fish and bringing back rum and molasses, and occasionally a slave. As late as 1773, there were in New Castle, in a population of six hundred and one, thirteen slaves, seven being men and six women. All the industries and prosperity in New Castle depended on the fisheries for more than two hundred years. One of the principal town officers was the "Culler of fish and staves." Both being exported were subject to inspection; the staves to a double inspection, for they returned hooped and filled with sweetness and potations, or as Poins says, "Sir John Sack and sugar."

The course of trade in this province was in this order: first, furs, or peltry; then lumber; and thirdly, fish.* And it must always be remembered that New Hampshire and Maine owed their first discovery and settlement to the trade in these products,

---

* The first seal adopted by New Hampshire, in 1776, represented two, if not all three, of these resources of the State. Why this seal, which is of exquisite workmanship, and probably by Paul Revere, should have been exchanged for the ugly thing now in use, is difficult to understand. Its motto was, and continues to be, most appropriate — *Vis Unita Fortior*.

and not to the desire for civil or religious freedom. The
colonists here were sent out by the "merchant adventurers" of
England in search of commodities, not places to worship God
after their own fashion. This fact has always given to the
people of this region a different character from that of Plymouth
and Massachusetts Bay, where alone could the declaration of
John Higginson of Salem, Mass., in 1663, be heard and believed:
"Let merchants, and such as are increasing cent per cent,
remember this, that worldly gain was not the end and design of
the people of New England, but religion. And if any man
among us make religion as twelve, and the world as thirteen,
such an one hath not the spirit of a true New England man."
The manner of conducting the fishing business in New Castle
was extremely simple; it was essentially barter; that is, the
owner of vessels usually kept a store, from which he fitted
them out, from which he also supplied the families of the fishermen with everything needed in their absence. So that a man
returning from a cruise would find usually that his accounts
were already balanced, often that he was in debt to the store, and
could only turn about and sail again. The domestic welcome
was brief and to the point — "How much have you made?"
and "When are you going again?" And so it went on till the
fisherman was an old man, or lost his life in those fatal gales
which so often sweep the Grand Banks. If he owned a house,
there was apt to be, in time, a mortgage upon it to the owner of
the vessels in which he sailed. There was very little cash in
circulation; if a man became possessed of any, he held on to it,
hid it, buried it, did anything with it except spend it. A gold
piece was an heir-loom, and was saved till death or a famine.
People raised wool and flax; carded, spun and wove them into
outer and inner clothing. Some expert dame cut and fashioned
the coats and gowns and was paid in yarn or cloth. Their bed-
cord was made from the inner bark of the elm. The shoemaker
came to the house or had a shop in his own, and shod the community, taking his pay in leather or fish. The schoolmaster and
minister were compensated much in the same manner. The
ministers of New Castle were distinguished men in their day, of
whom I shall write in another place; but only here notice their
equality with the community in worldly matters. They had a
house provided for them, and land alloted for a garden; they

had a cow and a slave, the good-will of the people, and occasionally a present from pious friends of the province, in England; but for the rest, their salary was paid in salt fish, which they in turn bartered for the necessities of life. And if the length of their sermons was proportioned to their emoluments, we must infer the latter to have been quite handsome. As in most other parts of New England, in early times, produce was the basis of exchange, so here fish paid for everything. The traditions and lore of the fisheries make the annals of New Castle instructive, as well as representative of much of the civil and domestic history of the whole coast of New England. The cod was not only useful and emblematic, but he was fashionable; and throughout New England, previous to the Revolution, among all classes, he was the king of the Saturday dinner-table. But we have dined upon him long enough now, and will pass on by his ancient domain, past the crumbling wharves and fish-houses and ghosts of tanned, storm-beaten skippers, into the way locally known as the "Cape Road." There are a few old houses upon one side of it; the other the water washes. The road comes to an end shortly, at the last house. Standing here, the view of the Piscataqua, the lower harbor, the western portion of the village, and Kittery side, are as good as can be obtained. In this picturesque little by-path one instinctively expects to see some romantic human form — and there she stands! The artist has drawn the Cape Road and the figure with the touch of genius. It is not a milk-maid; no, nor the "summer boarder." Should I, who know so well the swift stream and the dangerous rocks below the bank, venture to guess, it is the daughter of the Lorelei; she, whom the Lord of Appledore, sailing by, once saw; saw her signal, saw

> —"her white hand lifted
> Show like a waft of a sea-bird's wing;
>
> "I know her not and shall know her never,
> But ever I watch for that friendly sign;
> And up or down with the stately river
> Her lovely greeting is always mine."

If we should take the other branch of the way which brought us hither, it would lead by the site of the Walton house, which in 1682-83 was so much troubled by witches; and, finally to the Three Bridges crossing from island to island and landing in Portsmouth at Frame Point.

The only remaining relic of the Walton house, is a young sprout from the stump of a Lombardy poplar, that stood by its door. A brick is now and then turned up by the plough on the grounds. This house was long notorious in early times for the strange things which happened in and about it. The Devil was thought to be at the bottom of them. But witchcraft never flourished in the New Hampshire colony; no one suffered any extreme penalty on suspicion of it, though by the Province law it was a capital offence. It was only the echo of the delusions of Salem and Massachusetts Bay, which, being known here, created some natural excitement, and sudden apprehension of the supernatural in every unusual noise, or appearance, or occurrence; just as after listening to ghost stories at the end of the evening we go to bed fearfully, and readily believe our own house to be haunted. Here nothing serious came of the current frenzy, for the people were of a different stock and temperament from those of the neighboring colonies This Province had the distemper in a very mild form, without bloodletting. Most of the occurrences in connection with it were confined to New Castle; and concerning the most memorable of them, that which happened at the Walton house, on the road where we are now walking, I will give the reader a short story.

George Walton, though I cannot find that he was a regular inn-keeper, seems to have entertained, in the latter part of the seventeenth century, most of the royal officials either stationed here or visiting. Among them was Richard Chamberlain, royal secretary of the Province of New Hampshire. While Chamberlain was a guest in the domicile of Walton, the house and its occupants became the objects of the malice of evil spirits; or, as some said,—for there were unbelievers in those days,—of the animosity of a certain old woman, whom Walton had wronged in some transaction touching a certain parcel of land; while still others averred the strange proceedings nothing but the "waggery of unlucky boys." We have the whole history of the case from the pen of the guest of Walton, Richard Chamberiain, in a very rare pamphlet, published by him on his return to London, with the subjoined title-page:

>Lithobolia; or, the Stone-throwing Devil. Being an Exact and True Account (by way of Journal) of the various actions of infernal Spirits, or (Devils Incarnate) Witches, or both; and the great Disturbance and Amazement they gave to George Waltons Family, at a place called Great Island in the Province of New Hampshire in New England, chiefly in throwing about (by an Invisible hand) Stones, Bricks, and Brick-bats of all sizes, with several other things, as Hammers, Mauls, Iron-Crows, Spits, and other domestick Utensils, as came into their Hellish Minds, and this for the space of a Quarter of a Year. By R. C., Esq., who was a sojourner in the same Family the whole Time, and an Ocular Witness of those Diabolick Inventions. The Contents hereof being manifestly known to the Inhabitants of that Province, and Persons of other Provinces, and is upon record in his Majestie's Council Court held for that Province. 4to. Dedication 2, and pp. 16. London: Printed and are to be sold by E. Whitlook near Stationers-Hall. 1698.

I wish now I could quote the body of the pamphlet, since it is a very quaint narrative, full of realistic details, of parentheses and amplifications, all in that grave, ingenious style, so pleasing and illusive, which the old English chroniclers were wont to employ in the relation of marvels. The author appears to be quite as intent on inculcating the doctrine that witches and witchcraft exist, as in telling his particular instance; he wishes "to rectifie the depraved judgements and sentiments of disbelieving Persons," and says that his narrative will convince them of their error. It appears that the "stone-throwing devil" dealt rather gently by the writer, never hurting, only alarming him:

and stones rolled across the hall and in his room only when he sat down " to touch his little musical instrument." It is pleasing to note that he had music, books and pictures in his rooms. But others received "lapidary salutations" of a much more trying sort, so that their backs, shins and arms were black and blue. The stones varied in size from small pebbles (of which on one occasion a hatfull was picked up) to thirty pounds' weight. Some were hot, some cold; sometimes they shivered the windows, glass, lead and fastenings into flinders; at others into little squares of the size of a checker-board. Once one went through the glass, cutting a clean hole, like a bullet. These "stony Disturbances" were accompanied by "dismal whistlings," "snortings," and a trampling as of colts' feet. He finds by a strictly scientific process of numbering and marking such stones as he could recover, that the same ones were employed over and over by the witch; which might confirm the notion of the total depravity of inanimate matter, but must surely explode any theory of meteoric causes. These stones were handed about as fearful curiosities; but did no harm except on the premises of George Walton. There they spared neither the family, nor any curious chance visitor. People seem to have gone there on purpose to be pelted, or the usual foible of seeing for themselves. The Rev. Benj. Woodbridge, who was then the chief candlestick of the New Castle church, at sixty pounds a year, was hit; so was George Jaffrey, who built the Jaffrey Cottage; and the author thinks that Walton, whom the "stonery" pursued most, must have died from the effects. True, it was some years after the event that he died, but what so likely a cause? and afterward his estate went to pieces.

There were so many of these bewitched stones, and for so long a time flying about, that some of them must still be in the ground of the Walton estate; for in the long run, gravitation beats the levity out of the most enchanted as well as most ambitious stone. We want but little of a complete series of the relics of New Castle history, and I could wish we possessed some of those infested fragments of our rocky isle. Many persons did, at the time, preserve them as mementos of the affair. Capt. Walter Barefoot, Commander of the Fort, and sometime Judge and Lieutenant-Governor of the Province, owned one that had played a conspicuous part at the Walton house: "a good flat stone," but which rolled about as if it had neither corner nor edge, resembling the airy globe made by spinning a ring swiftly. But stones were not the only objects that suddenly shook off their inertia; hammers, pewter pots, the andirons and candlesticks, sun dials, joint-stools, hetchels and hoes, left their humble drudgery and pirouetted over the floors and ceilings, kicking out whatever legs or handles they could muster, with all the abandonment of a ballet girl. The spit went up the chimney; and the haycocks were found in the tops of the apple-trees. One of the singular features of the nocturnal manifestations was that a black cat could be seen usually at the very moment. And this black cat plays a prominent part in one other witchcraft on record in the town, the "case of Susanna Trimmings," which I shall relate when we reach the spot where it happened.

Goodman Walton and his family were almost distracted, and the town was stirred to its depths: some prayed continually, others scoffed, and everybody gossiped. Distinguished men from other provinces came to New Castle to see the wonders; and they reached the ear of Cotton Mather and were set down in his famous book. It was the opinion of the pious and learned that they were "venefical operations," "contrivances and combinations of the old Serpent." How to combat them?—that was the difficult question. We know how it was answered in Massachusetts—with a rope; and in other times and places with torture and fire and all kinds of judicial murder, and almost everywhere by supplications and sermons. But in New Castle, at the time of these occurrences, according to the author of this account, they proceeded to cast out the witch by an incantation which seems equally fitted to raise one. It was thus: "August 1. On Wednesday the window in my ante-chamber was broke again, and many stones were plaid about, abroad, and in the house, in the daytime, and at night. The same day in morning they tried this experiment: they did set on the fire a pot with urine, and cooked pins in it, with design to have it boil, and by that means to give punishment to the witch or wizard, (that might be the wicked Procurer or Contriver of this stone affliction) and take off theirs; as they had been advised. This was the effect of it: As the liquor began to grow hot, a stone came and broke the top or mouth of it, and threw it down, and spilt what was in it; which being made good again, another

stone, as the pot grew hot again, broke the handle off; and being
recruited (*sic!*) and filled the third time, was then with a stone
quite broke to pieces and split, and so the operation became
frustrate and fruitless."

The wizard continued to have the best of it for a month or
two more, in spite of prayers, maledictions and pins. At last
the excitement ceased, though the matter was canvassed long
afterward. The Walton house got itself new windows and the
stones settled down into their accustomed apathy, contented to
be no higher than a wall, and only magical when built into the
tower of some poet.

Chamberlain concludes his testimonial concerning the "stone-
throwing devil" with the following doctrinal application :

"Who, that peruses these præternatural occurrences can pos-
sibly be so much an Enemy to his own Soul, and irrefutable
Reason, as obstinately to oppose himself to, or confusedly fluct-
uate in, the Opinion and doctrine of Demons, and Spirits and
Witches: certainly he that do's so, must do two things more: He
must temerariously unhinge, or undermine the best Religion in
the World; and he must disingenuously quit and abandon that
of the three Theologick Virtues or Graces, to which the great
Doctor of the Gentiles gave the precedence, Charity, through his
unchristian and uncharitable Incredulity."

Charity, forsooth! It were better to have that which thinketh
no evil; and for us, that charity which is provoked only to smiles
at the solemn antics of our ancestors. According to Cotton
Mather (for there is no year date in Chamberlain's pamphlet
except that of its publication in London) the "stone-throwing
devil" began his tricks in New Castle, June 11th. 1682, and appears
to have continued them for about three months. This was the
exact period when New Castle saw its most anxious days, prior to
the Revolution. For Cranfield ruled over the people; a governor
who was in league with the Mason heirs to assert their title to
all the lands here, whether occupied or not, and who attempted
to extort quit-rents of all holders. Now, though the settlers had
not strictly taken their holdings by the primitive form of "turf
and twig," yet they had been for a generation or two in peaceable
possession. The prospect of a system of tenantry like that of
England, or of ejectment. which already had been carried out
successfully upon one prominent citizen of New Castle (George

Jaffrey) weighed heavily upon their minds. And there was another trouble brewing, equally oppressive. Though never Puritans after the manner of some of their neighbors, their form of church service was essentially Congregational; that good old faith which led on to civil freedom, and under whose teaching and encouragments the battles of the Revolution were fought. But Cranfield was of the established English Church, and wanted to root out the growing heresies of this Province; either that, or else in some way that we cannot now fathom, the personal interests of himself and his friends induced him to take active measures toward changing the religious rites of the churches here.

He demanded of the Rev. Joshua Moody, the minister of Portsmouth, the sacraments according to the customary English form. Moody was recalcitrant, and Cranfield resolute; the latter had the power, but Moody the popular voice and sympathy. The contest came to an issue, and Moody was apprehended, brought to New Castle for trial and sentenced to six months' imprisonment in New Castle prison, where the "irons called bilbose are exceeding large, an inch over, five feet and several inches long." During this time, his flock in Portsmouth nearly perished for the want of religious ministrations. Indeed, one poor soul did die in consequence — so saith the record: "Good Mrs. Martin was buried, being not able to live above one Sabbath after the shutting up the doors of the sanctuary."

This is the lament of one William Vaughan, concerning the same affair: "Our minister lies in prison, and a famine of the word of God is coming upon us. No public worship, no preaching of the Word! What ignorance, profaneness and misery must needs ensue!"

One other event in the Province at this period added to the general excitement: an insurrection against the government of Cranfield, under the leadership of Edward Gove of Hampton and nine other men. They were all arrested, brought to New Castle, here tried, and the chief conspirator, Gove, sentenced for high treason: the only conviction of that kind in New Hampshire history, as the imprisonment of Moody was the first case of religious persecution in New England. It was adjudged that Gove should be hung, cut down before dead, his bowels be burnt before his face, his head cut off and his body quartered;

none of which sentence, we are glad to write, was executed. He lived to be shut up in the Tower of London some years; then to return to his farm in Hampton, where he lived to much multiply his name in that precinct. He lived, but complained that he suffered from poison secretly administered while a prisoner at New Castle.

To crown all, they had only just recovered from a terrible fright by the flight of a comet through their heavens.* This, in fact, had created such consternation that a public fast had been called, to propitiate by prayer and self-abasement, the heavenly powers. The proclamation gives three reasons for a day of fasting and supplication: the sickness of the President of the Province, John Cutts; "in respect of that *awful portentous blazing star*, usually foreboding some calamity to the

beholder thereof;" and the third reason is mysterious, but very curious: "also having a real sympathy with the *great thoughts of heart* in our brothers and neighbors." I have somewhat anticipated a portion of the town annals, in order to picture the condition and temper of this community when the "stone-throwing devil" entered upon the scene to intensify the excitement already existing.

New Castle was the focus of whatever happened in the Province at that time, for here lived the Governor and his officials; here were held the councils and the courts of law; it was the port of entry; here was the prison for the whole Province, and

---

* Prof. E. C. Pickering, of the Cambridge Observatory, informs me that this was the comet known as the "Comet of 1680," still visible in 1681. It is supposed to be the same as that of 1843, 1880 and 1882.

the fort or castle, its stronghold, under command of Capt. Walter Barefoot, the most interesting figure of the period. The town must have been a lively place to live in during those years, with its witchcraft doings, its comet, its ejectments, the hated Governor, and prison full of traitors and ministers in danger of London Tower, of the gallows, or secret poisoning. One can hardly realize that this peaceful and tranquil island, where now nothing ever happens more remarkable than a shipwreck or the building of a new house, was abounding formerly in stirring events.

We are proud of our past; we grew out of it and stand upon it; and though our affairs are now so small and obscure, it is but the last page in our annals, which has a new and deeper interest when we turn back and read up to it. This insular life is good and sweet; full of contentment, humble services, sufferings and joys.

Our affairs are of little consequence to the world, but concern us greatly and are measured or magnified to our need — "*parva sed apta nobis.*"

Our natural boundaries, wholly of ocean and river, separate and circumscribe our interests, give a certain local color to life, an idiomatic flavor to speech, and a maritime direction to all thought and imagination. This, if you are a dweller or visitor here, though neither fisherman nor sailor, I reckon an advantage, not only for entertainment, but in the studies and practices of intellectual life, and the exercise of all duties owed to the community. It is pleasant to feel you have not got the universe to deal with this time, but only some six hundred acres.

Fixed and faithful to these, the great world in time passes by this way, bringing whatever your dreams have fostered and destiny, with its cubit and rein, predetermined that you shall possess or be denied. Thus you cannot rise to dangerous heights; nor can you fall low, for, like the little spider, a trusty rope is always in your hand.

Let us walk on from the site of the "stone-throwing devil" house, where we have lingered too long, to the Three Bridges. On the highest point of the hill which we pass just before coming to them, was a small earthwork of Revolutionary date. It was never used, and is now almost level with the ground. At the time of its construction there were no houses opposite.

and it commanded a narrow part of the river, between the northwestern end of New Castle and Seavy's Island, on which was a companion work, Fort Sullivan. The view from here takes in the sea, most of the islands in the harbor, the whole of Kittery, namely, "Kittery Foreside," "Backside" and "Kittery Point," and we see the way at least to the extreme eastern end of the town, which Mrs. Celia Thaxter calls "Kittery Cutt." Yonder is the queer old Fort McClary at Kittery Point, a nondescript structure, half wood, half stone, and many-angled; something between a block-house and Martello tower. A little distance eastward of it is the mansion of Sir William Pepperell, and his tomb. Sir William Pepperell was a trader, and the son of a trader; a militia colonel, rich, prosperous, a man of probity and sagacity, and the central human figure in these parts, in the first half of the eighteenth century. In the French war, 1745, he was selected to lead an expedition against the citadel of Louisburg, called in its day "the Dunkirk of America." This expedition is the most amusing affair in American history; it was the first regularly organized military enterprise of Yankee soldiers, and showed thus early all their peculiar characteristics. Pepperell was selected, in the first place, on account of his *popularity;* and the soldiers accompanying him had all the inventive, independent and frolicksome traits exhibited in our latest war. It was a regular picnic, holiday muster, or, as described at the time, by the current synonym for fun, "a Cambridge Commencement." Only those who remained at home took the business seriously; one of these, a little before the expedition sailed, nearly ruined the enterprise, which had been planned in secret, by being unable to restrain himself at family prayers. But Whitefield, the great preacher, had given it his blessing and a motto, *Nil desperandum Christo duce.* It was successful mainly through the energy of Lieutenant-Colonel William Vaughan,* of Portsmouth, a dauntless man, who could see no obstacle in the track of his intention. But Pepperell had the glory, and was made the first American Baronet. Kittery Point is full of his departed fame and name.

---

* Voltaire, in Préces de l' Histoire de Louis XV, gives to Vaughan the credit of proposing the expedition. Un négociant, nommé Vaughan, propose à ses concitoyens de la nouvelle Angle-terre de lever des troupes pour assiéger Louisbourg. Chap. XXVIII.

Beside his own mansion, there are several others associated with his family: the Bray house, built 1660; the Sparhawk house, of noble proportions and style; and the Cutts house, the scene of enough tragedies in one family to furnish out an annual novelist. There is a way by water from the Kittery side of the harbor, through Chauncy Creek to Brayboat Harbor, on the main sea. It is the pleasantest in the world — so it seems when one is there, or when remembered. It has varied scenery: high banks, woods, marsh, two ancient bridges, one of which was formerly a drawbridge, for security, and at the end are groves of walnut-trees bravely growing close to the salt Atlantic.

> " Down to the surf the fearless little wood,
> Childlike it smiles in all the Atlantic's roar."

Near these trees is the cairn of Francis Champernowne, an adventurer of the early colonial days; a man of Norman and royal descent, who had his mansion here, his mill and his drawbridge. The entrance and outlet of the creek are wide; but in the middle part it narrows to the beam of a boat, though still deep, and in all its course the water is crystal clear. Along the shores memories and names abide: the Cutts, Pepperells, Chauncys and Champernownes; their tide has ebbed; but the sea continues to bring back the flood, which you must take if you would explore the creek and review its old and slumbering memorials. The higher banks are crowned with the most diminutive houses in all this region; each with its small garden, and its boat-landing, where children are always at play. The houses look just their size, and you wonder if they are not the pigmy people who built and inhabit them. At least you would fancy so, unless you should happen to enter one of them and find men and women of good stature and comeliness, living with cheerful simplicity in their tidy nests. You will have a cup of water, freshly drawn, their best word, and you will not go away without some flowers from the terrace border; and going, you will think of the old proverb, " God oft hath a great share in a little house." But your sailor and your fisherman, though dealing so much with the spacious floor of the sea and an unwalled world, dearly love to creep into small houses and rooms, like their sea-cabins and forecastles. They want little space for their feet, but much for their eyes.

Returning from Chauncy Creek, and rounding with your boat the small, rocky promontories all along "Kittery Side," you enter Spruce Creek, which runs up through the land into York. It is broad at the entrance, and soon widens still more; but, like most ocean inlets, it does not fulfill its promising invitation, and terminates shortly in marsh and mud. A salt-water creek must be taken like your affairs, at the flood. At the ebb it looks like a street in ruins; all is naked that should be covered; all is blackened, haggard and desolate. In another six hours, when it begins to swell and fill from "the impulse of the outer sea," the change is magical. The long, slender eel-grass that lay flat and motionless in the bed of the creek, begins to wave as if a soft west wind were blowing over it. The stream grows swifter; it hurries on; it has a message from the ocean, an appointment to keep, and for only a brief space. The ledges, smooth and blanched by millions of tides, wait to be kissed; and the trees bend down for the low, cool breeze, which twice a day the tide brings from the deep and salutary recesses of the ocean, as a boon to all the neighboring shores. It stays at the flood but a little while; the water-line on the stones soon shows that it is making ready to retreat; then you must turn your prow and drift homeward. Oars are superfluous; hardly will you need the helm; the creek knows the way. Let it command, while you meditate.

There are four creeks making out of the waters which surround New Castle: Spruce, Chauncy, Seavy and Sagamore. Two of them, Spruce and Chauncy, are from the river side; Seavy and Sagamore from Little Harbor, which itself is only a more spacious creek, but breaking through the land, at length, and uniting itself with the river by three inlets, over which cross the Three Bridges. The waters here are full of small islands, green to the tide in summer, and in autumn a blaze of red. The first bridge lands on one of these, called Goat Island; the second starts from the latter and lands on Shapley's Island; and the third bridge crosses from Shapley's to Frame Point, in the southern part of Portsmouth.

At the last bridge are still committed, every day, the boldest highway robberies, and it is necessary for the unwary foot-passenger to arm himself with a three-barrelled gun, loaded with the smallest denomination of "shot" made at the United States mint. I blush for this chartered relic of feudalism; but the blame is not upon New Castle. We long ago, and when much less prosperous than at present, offered to free the portion of the bridges within our territory; that is, nearly to the western end of the middle bridge. But our worthy Portsmouth neighbors are conservative, and would rather shut their shops than anyone should break into their town by other than the ancient ways. Yet they are fond of coming to New Castle, and so we built them a new, free bridge by a pleasant way, over Little Harbor, to the southern side of the town and Wentworth Hotel. We hope, in time, to wean them from their ancient habit of gathering and paying tolls at their barriers. But the gateman of the three bridges now keeps them in such excellent repair, and his own domicile on the pier, and its grounds, are so neat and tasteful, that one almost involuntarily gives up his purse, and says, with that dear old highwayman, Falstaff, "'tis no sin for a man to labor in his vocation." Besides, we can have a look at his inventions; for he is the inventor of I know not what ingenious machines; an anchor, almost equal to Hope's, that will hold or loosen itself on any bottom; a water bicycle, which resembles, more than anything else, those great water spiders in the still places of a brook; and there is, on the last bridge, his floating aquarium, full of all the common and uncommon fish of these waters, which you enter through a veranda where summer refreshments are served; so that you are quite likely to forget the offensive threepenny fine — "Take, gateman, thrice thy fee," — especially if you have observed and enjoyed the variety of land and water scenery to be had from each of the bridges. On the right hand are Clark's, Seavy's and Peirce's islands; on Seavy's is the Revolutionary earthwork, Fort Sullivan; and on Peirce's, Fort Washington, of the same date. Behind Seavy's Island, but in view of the bridges, is the United States Navy Yard. The most conspicuous object now at its piers is the old frigate Constitution. She has had a house of one story built over her entire deck, and with her chunky bow and square stern she reminds one of the ark of his childhood. From the bridges is a good view of the older portion of Portsmouth; that portion first named and known as Strawberry Bank. On some one of the

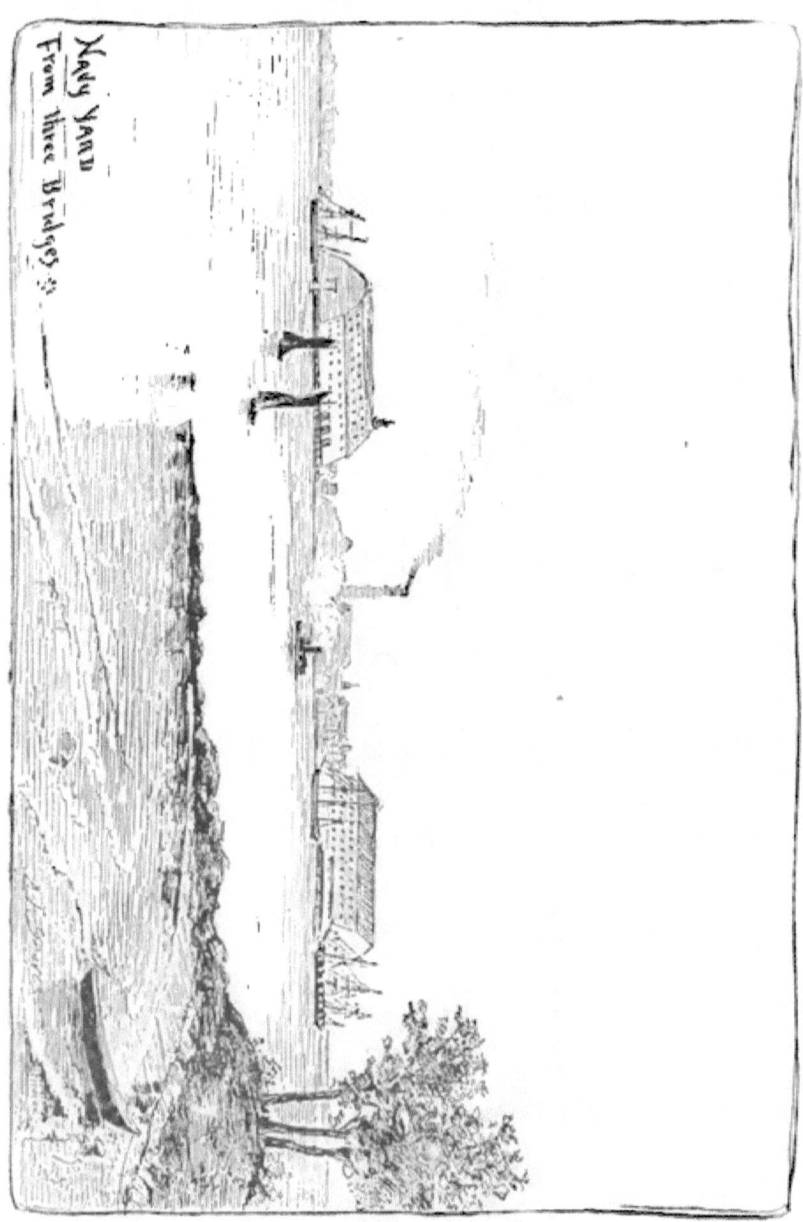

islands off this side of Portsmouth, in 1690, was built probably the first war-vessel in this country, the Falkland, a fifty-four-gun ship, for the British government. In passing over the first and second bridges, we see the swiftest and most dangerous mile of the Piscataqua. Here the pilot must be wary and experienced; and he is quite likely to do some swearing at "Pull-and-be-damned Point." His predecessors of old christened it, and he but confirms it.

The Piscataqua is hardly a river; it is rather an arm of the sea. Its total length is scarcely twenty miles, and it is salt, though several small streams of fresh water empty into it. A few miles west of Portsmouth it spreads into a broad bay, covering some twelve thousand acres. The name Piscataqua, or Pascataqua, is an Abnaquian Indian word, meaning "the [tidal] river branches." Discovered in 1603, by Martin Pring, and perhaps earlier, in 1524, by Verazzano, an Italian sailor, re-discovered in 1614 by Capt. John Smith, it had an early importance as being the chief eastern boundary between the New England colonists and their constant enemies, the French and their Indian allies. So it came about that, for a long period, all this region on both sides of the river, and inland to its headwaters, bore the general name in England, and in the adjacent colonies of "Piscattaway," or "Pascattaway," from the name of the river. I find the name spelled in seven forms; the correct Indianese is supposed to be Piscataquack, and when so written it refers to the place or land where the river divides; that is, to the territory about the junction of the Salmon and Cocheco rivers. For the Indians seldom generalized a name for natural objects, but designated them at a given point, or from a particular feature; so that a river might have several names along its course : as at its junction with another stream, or at a favorite fishing, hunting or camping ground. If Piscataqua were divided and accented thus — Pis-câ-tâ′-quâ — it would be a fine sounding word, worthy of its historic and romantic associations.

Nothing in our day is seen upon its waters so picturesque and foreign looking as the *gundaloes*, which creep along the shores and in and out among the islands. They have one short, stumpy mast, and a very long yard, rigged with a lateen sail. The yard is held to the mast by a chain hooked into an iron band around

the yard, and rove through a sheave-hole in the mast-head; thus
enabling it to swing horizontally, when passing under bridges, or
when at anchor. The gundalow is at its best for a picture when
lying on some tide-deserted beach, its yard on a line with the
deck, and the sail loosely brailed up. It will be noticed in the
"Onward," (for which, as well the description, I am indebted
to Capt. W. H. Treadwell) that the yard is weighted at the forward end, in order, when lowering, to balance the weight of the
sail, which is mainly aft of the mast. I have of late years seen
so many illustrations and paintings of the gundalow of the
Piscataqua, and always incorrect, that I determined in this book
to give one page to a realistic likeness. Those who want their

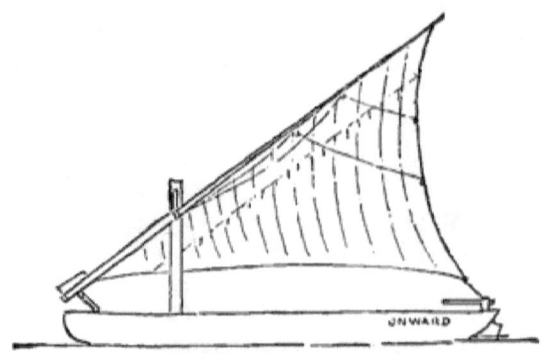

PISCATAQUA GUNDALOW
DRAWN by Capt. W. H. TREADWELL

gundalow with sauce can turn to page fifty-eight. Their lading is
usually brick, sand or gravel, stone, coal or any rough cargo,
carried on deck. The gundalow is the humble sister of the sloop
on one side, and first, but aristocratic, cousin to the skow on the
other; a craft indigenous here, and adapted to our much
bebridged waters. Its name and rig probably came from Italy,
though the one has been corrupted and the other transformed.
Gundalows have been in use on the river for many generations, and once were quite elegant in their appointments, carrying passengers as well as freight. Those were the days when
Gov. James Sullivan, of Massachusetts, served his apprentice-
ship on one of them, and learned to use the helm and the sweep.
I have found an allusion to gundalows as far back as 1696;

and an important one in 1726; which gives, as I believe, the nearly correct orthography, shows also their general use thus early, and incidentally discovers the beginning of a long contest over the building of a bridge across Little Harbor, which New Castle wanted, and which Rye and Portsmouth opposed. I will quote a paragraph from the petition of the two latter towns, in which the name appears; and where is shown also our forefathers' manner of dealing with language when they designed to make it especially emphatic and convincing.

"Another unspeakable hardship which will attend a bridge is ye transportation of Hay from ye meadows and marishes where the tides must be attended both by night and day; and to pass under a draw bridge or through any such gap as their may be with a GONDELA of hay in a dark night and a strong wind or in any other vessel with so strong a current as there is besides must needs be a danger too terrible to be thought on."

You may decline this word: gondola, gondela, gundalow; the first form is pure, the second a variation, the third a corruption. And this order shows also another sort of declension, in the uses to which the craft was put: first, a conveyance for passengers only; second, a similar purpose and sometimes also freight; and last, nothing but rough cargoes of coal and ballast. Words are corrupted as fast as the thing signified comes to an abased use. One of the earliest names in New Castle history was John Amazeen, called sometimes John the Greek, sometimes John the Italian. I conjecture that he it was who christened the "gondela;" and perhaps suggested her rig from the xebecs and feluccas of his own native seas.

On the left of the Three Bridges are the various branches of Little Harbor, dotted with islands. The largest, of forty acres, is called Leach's Island; it was the slave's quarter in Gov. Benning Wentworth's time, being directly opposite his mansion. Among the smaller ones are Pest, Clampit, Snuff-Box, etc. All the islands east of the main channel of Little Harbor belong to New Castle. The only deep water on the left of the Three Bridges is near the middle one, and is known as "The Pool." Here a French fleet anchored for three months in 1782. At the turn of Little Harbor toward the sea, and just where it seems to end in that direction, almost overhanging the water, is the old Governor Wentworth mansion. We shall see this nearer when we go up Sagamore creek, and then we will rest on our oars a moment. From the middle bridge, it appears a pile of buildings, of fantastic shapes, embosomed in trees and shrubbery.

Returning by the way we came, we may take the upper, or principal thoroughfare of New Castle village, passing two school-houses (in one of which is the Town Hall) and two churches, which make up our public buildings. The Congregational Church is the third building occupied by the society since its organization, about the middle of the seventeenth century. The first structure was in the neighborhood of Fort Constitution; the next, directly in front of the present. The church has a pretty flower-garden attached, laid out and fondly tended by the last settled minister, Rev. Lucius Alden. Being a bachelor, his flowers were to him as wife and children. When I relate the internal history of New Castle, I shall better give what concerns this church.

Now, as we walk on, we enter the road which leads by Wentworth Hotel to the new free bridge. Nearly all the distance the ocean is in sight. There are no special objects to point out that we shall not have a fairer view of from the eminence on which the Wentworth stands. Yet, as I wish to recover and preserve as many of the ancient designations of particular localities in New Castle as I can, I will here record that the land now wooded and enclosed between the entrance to Jaffrey Point and the next open field on the south was testified to by Sampson Sheafe, in 1707, as always known to him by the name of "Lux, his Field." There is no howsoever small parcel of land, or shore, or little hill, or back-yard in New Castle but has its prescriptive title, or sometimes nickname. And I find that it was always the fashion here; and that consequently there are often several names by which to identify, and sometimes confuse, places, as something would give rise, in the course of generations, to a new name, while the older one still lingered on in deeds and tradition. The views on the right of the way we are now traversing are terminated by hill and forest. The higher of the hills, and one of the highest in New Castle, is known as Bos'n Hill. The tradition is that it received its name from a certain boatswain in early times who hung himself there to a pine tree, and that when a storm is brewing his whistle begins to be heard, and increases in loudness with the tempest.

BOS'N HILL.

(A NEW CASTLE, N. H., LEGEND.)

The wind blows wild on Bos'n Hill,
    Far off is heard the ocean's rote;
Low overhead the gulls scream shrill,
    And homeward scuds each little boat.

Then the dead Bos'n wakes in glee
    To hear the storm-king's song;
And from the top of mast-pine tree
    He blows his whistle loud and long.

The village sailors hear the call,
    Lips pale and eyes grow dim;
Well know they, though he pipes them all,
    He means but one shall answer him.

He pipes the dead up from their graves,
    Whose bones the tanzy hides;
He pipes the dead beneath the waves,
    They bear and cleave the rising tides.

But sailors know when next they sail
    Beyond the Hilltop's view,
There 's one amongst them shall not fail
    To join the Bos'n's crew.

Anyone who guesses me to be either historian or antiquarian will be compelled to guess again; or, if he chance to read this little volume, he will not need to guess at all. Yet I may be pardoned for introducing some of the ambitious phrases of history, in describing New Castle as having had three notable historic periods; or, a rise and decline, and again a rise. The first period extended from the settlement of the country to the Revolution; the second, of decline, from the Revolution to the Centennial year; and the third begins with the building of Wentworth Hotel, in 1874, and the free bridge in 1875; in all about two hundred and fifty years. The hotel and bridge mark the returning tide of prosperity; which, so to speak, is a land tide; that is, it is from that side, which sends us every year larger numbers of guests. Some of them become attached, and, building houses, become residents; others, coming for a summer to the Wentworth Hotel, return to it year after year. It was not so much business as admiration of the situation that moved the first builder of this house. Indeed, his enthusiasm was deeper than his purse. Like so many other American enterprises, where the roof falls upon the head of him who raises it first, the founder of the Wentworth Hotel never himself reaped any benefit. It seems almost everything must needs fail once, often several times, before it becomes a real and permanent success. We sow and never reap, and we reap where we have not sown. On that side of the road where the Wentworth Hotel and its various annexes now stand, was a pine grove; the house was planted in the midst of it; the trees overshadowed the piazzas, and several were allowed to grow up through them. At first, this primitive order of things was much admired. But suddenly some one discovered that, lolling in an easy-chair or hammock, the views were obstructed. From that moment the fate of the beautiful grove was decreed. There is no good American who has not laid his axe at the root of some tree, and generally forest. Piece by piece the wood fell, according to the whim of successive landlords, or wish of some distinguished guest, who thought if certain trees were removed there would be uncovered a prettier picture. So the low, evergreen veil was torn away; all but a corner, and a fringe along the bank of the water. Its site has been replaced by fine lawns and terraces; and by the planting of trees on other parts of the grounds the wood gods are appeased. At the foot of the grove is a piece of ancient road, which formerly was the way from an old bridge across Little Harbor, from Blunt's Island, into the northern portion of New Castle. Along its route are many cellar-holes, old pear-trees, and the only living spring I know of here; but not a single house. This road passed Long Point and Bos'n Hill, and finally reached the village in a circuitous manner. No part of it is now a public highway. But the foot-passenger may trace it out and find a short cut from

"Frost Fields"

the southern side of the island to the Three Bridges, by a very pretty lover's lane. At the end of this lane the last house of the whole way was pulled down a few years since. A pear-tree, which must be two centuries old, is there, a venerable house-mark.

Let us return to the hill on which the Wentworth Hotel stands. It is here I wish to tempt you by taking you up into a high tower and offering you a world. I know of no spot where one is so likely to yield. The very least you will do will be to accept it for a season; and that is enough, it settles the business; you will come again, and ultimately it will triumph over all preferences. This is the experience of many chance visitors at New Castle. From the towers of Wentworth Hotel nearly the whole of Rockingham County can be seen, a portion of Strafford County, and of York County in Maine. The general name of the elevations on the west, that form, at the average distance of thirty miles, the horizon line, is the Blue Hills. A not very distinctive name, and generally employed most by those who see them at distance. Those living nearer have other, more definite names. These western hills are in color a rather lighter, softer blue than is common. I have been told by a countryman that it is due to the spruce forests with which they are mostly clothed. It may be so, for the leaf of the spruce is bluer than that of other evergreen trees. And, moreover, the hills are directly opposite the sun; the forests reflect the full light of it, and are less in shadow than Agamenticus on the north, which is much deeper in color. Everywhere along the sea-shore the effects of light are various and wonderful. All colors and shadows are intensified. The sea acts as a vast mirror; and the dense air is an artist who softens or heightens all objects. I should say he took the white out of everything as the preliminary of his art. Here, a new shingle looks, the first season, a generation old. If you want an old house at once, build it by the sea; and if you wish to remain young, live in it. Your face grows brown, but that is all; it is merely to bring you into harmonious coloring with the nature in which you are planted.

The summits of the Blue Hills bear particular names: as Teneriffe in Milton, Pawtuckaway in Nottingham, Saddleback in Deerfield. On the north are Bonnebeag in Berwick, and Agamenticus in York. These last are not more than fifteen miles

distant. Agamenticus was called, in the early times, Accomintacus and Aquamenticus, and gave its name to the country and English settlements in its neighborhood. It is closely associated with Passaconoway, the greatest Indian sachem in the eastern part of New England in the seventeenth century. He was a great warrior, and an equally great and frequent peacemaker. He foresaw the future, foreboded it, too, for his race, and warned his tribes, but counselled them to make friends of the white men. He himself made many treaties with them. This is his autograph, affixed to some of them, — his *totem*, he called it — 8.*
He was a most sagacious sachem — it almost seems as if those words were of the same derivation — and was believed by all his tribes to have supernatural powers. He could, at any rate, make water burn and re-clothe the leafless tree. In vain, however, did he try to turn back the tide of Englishmen, although he used every enchantment diligently. Water would burn, but would not run up hill. He knew it, at last, and would not fight against fate, and counselled peace and fraternity. The most remarkable story connected with him is that, under the name of St. Aspenquid, he visited every tribe of North American Indians, preaching the gospel of peace with the white men. And there is still celebrated, in some parts of New Brunswick, the Feast of St. Aspenquid.

His death was dramatic as his life had been. When a century old, he gathered all his tribes together upon the summit of Mt. Agamenticus, made a long feast of more than three thousand birds and beasts, spoke his short farewell words of wisdom and sadness, and disappeared, like a god, in a cloud and thunder. The manuscript of his address is missing. Cotton Mather's great waste-basket should have gathered it in, but he had his preferences, chiefly for the witchcraft of white Christians. The substance of it, however, is said to be on record. I have seen it, methinks; the lines are not as long as Walt Whitman's, nor as catalectic as Hiawatha.

This is the only Indian myth I know of, associated with the mountain peaks here to be seen; and Pawtuckaway appears to be the only other Indian name borne by any of them. Teneriffe is ambitious, but borrowed. As the settlers here were nearly

---

* He had several; this was his official totem.

all from the west of England, we should rather expect to find some mountain-peak with *pen* or *ben* in its name; but I know of none. The western hills I am now describing appear ten miles from the shore, as they do from the Wentworth towers. They are of the greatest use to the mariner, and especially to the off-shore fishermen, who set their trawls and deep sea lines by their bearings; and who distinguish them by a nomenclature of their own. At sea, Mt. Agamenticus is in the foreground, in solitary grandeur; it seems more lofty, having no companions for comparison. At its foot dwells a little community of basket makers and charcoal burners, with manners and customs of their own. I am afraid they need the services of the "Society for the propagation of the Gospel." They are the last fragment of the wreck of the city and bishopric of Gorgiana. Themselves and their teams are the most unique spectacle ever seen on the Portsmouth Parade, or market-place. The bodies of their carts are of the rudest home-made contrivance; the wheels are castaways, still whole only by some inherent property of a circle that lasts long and falls altogether (always, indeed, if you are poor enough, holding out another year) and drawn by what was once, perhaps, a horse, or, sometimes, a scrubby, stunted cow. Excellent subjects for genre artists, in painting or literature; and let us hope they will discover them before the "Society for the propagation of the Gospel." At home, you will find them gathering small birch wood or maple for their charcoal pits; or braying out basket splinthes from the wood of the black ash. For this operation they have a special word. Their baskets are of the coarser sort. They have not the skill or the art of the degenerate Indian, who understands how to make a basket that will sell itself, of beautiful form and colors, and perfumed with sweet-scented vernal grass.

In clear weather you may discern from the Wentworth towers Mount Washington, due north and ninety miles away. To find it, look a little to the right of the Navy Yard shears. There it looms, and you seem to be looking over into another world, especially in winter, when it rises like the white shoulder of some other planet.

On the northeast stretches the coast-line of Maine, beginning with Gerrish Island. Just off the southern end of this island is Whale's Back Light, the outer harbor light. It is in 43° 03′ north latitude, 70° 41′ west longitude; has a fixed white light, varied by flashes every minute and a half, and a fog-signal. The lens apparatus is of the fourth order, and the light is visible thirteen nautical, or sixteen common, miles. Opinions differ as to how far the fog-signal can be heard; it depends upon atmospheric conditions. Our sailors and fishermen say there are times when it is impossible to tell the direction of the sound, or its distance away. The tower is sixty-nine feet in height, of unhewn granite, starting from a ledge under water. This ledge is the continuation of the southern point of Gerrish Island, and it runs on another dangerous mile, then ends abruptly at Kitt's Rock, on which is a bell-buoy. Entering the harbor, you keep the buoy and light on the starboard. On the port side is the mouth of Little Harbor, marked on the left with that same spar-buoy which is the initial letter of this book, and on the right by a spindle; next, are Jaffrey Point, Elm Tree Cove, whose sightly cottage is shown on the next page, and Fort Point light, which, as soon as you have cleared, you are in a commodious and sheltered harbor, where your weary keel may rest with fourteen fathoms of cable at a secure anchor.

Whale's Back light was established in 1829. The man is still living who lit its lamp for the first time, Mr. Allen Porter. He lighted it at mid-day, and for one afternoon the sun at New Castle had few worshippers. Now only at sunset does it receive the torch of day, and hold it steadily aloft, alike through serene or dark, tempestuous nights, until a flashing hand comes out of the ocean and seizes it again. In 1872 Whale's Back light was rebuilt. The substruction of the old tower is left; and the handle of a dasher that you see sticking up through an old-fashioned red churn, is the fog-signal. The three together form a striking object in the seaward view.

Ten miles to the eastward, and far enough from the shore to illuminate the entire horizon, is Boon Island lighthouse. It stands upon a bare rock, in mid-ocean. The light is a beautiful, fixed, white one of the second class. The tower is one hundred and thirty-three feet in height. Here the keepers are imprisoned for most of the winter season, as it is difficult to launch a boat except in calmest weather, and always uncertain whether you can land on returning. Therefore, the keepers, of whom

WHALESBACK LIGHT.

there are three, with their women and children, must make careful provision for every contingency. They must nurse their own sick, and make accurate calculations that no other kind of nursing fall upon the winter time. A small light has recently been established at York Nubble, invisible from the Wentworth.

Looking directly seaward from the Wentworth towers, the Isles of Shoals are in view. They are at an average distance of six miles from the mainland. Appledore and Star are the principal islands; but there are five or six smaller ones, the best known of which are Duck, Smutty-Nose, Londoners, and White. Some of them are in Maine, others in New Hampshire. The division line leaves Appledore and Smutty-Nose on the left, and in Maine; all to the right are in New Hampshire. The Isles of Shoals light, eighty-seven feet in height and of the second class, is on White Island, the southwestern one of the group. It is a flashing red-and-white light, dear in the memory of all lovers of poets and verse, because once lighted and tended by a child of the muse.

> "I lit the lamps in the lighthouse tower,
> For the sun dropped down and the day was dead;
> They shone like a glorious clustered flower,—
> Ten golden and five red."

There is a light on the north end of Plum Island, at the entrance to Newburyport harbor, and also a small one at Ipswich harbor Southeast are the Cape Ann lights, on Thatcher's Island. The lamps are in two stone towers, one hundred and sixty-five and a half feet in height, eight hundred and ninety-five feet apart. They are lights of the first-class; and though thirty miles away, are usually visible — twin stars that never change their place throughout the night watches.

These are the lamp-posts that light the wide, silent pathways of our waters; and they are equally friendly to the dweller by the shores, guiding his belated footsteps by their cheerful gleam. The stars must pay the penalty of their splendor and height; while these humble, low-hung sentinels are faithful, in gloom and tempest, to ocean and to shore.

There is much of history and story connected with Boon Island, White Island and Thatcher's Island lighthouses, for which we must refer the reader to other writers. Wrecks are constantly happening in spite of our well-lighted coast. To each one there are tales of bravery and suffering. Thanks to the Life-Saving Service, these narratives are now collated and printed in full in its reports, and are extremely interesting.

The waters, from the mouth of the Piscataqua to Cape Ann, are commonly known as Ipswich bay. A bent arm represents the coast-line of the bay; and Ipswich lies in the elbow. On this side, that is, between the Piscataqua and Ipswich, are the Hampton and Rye beaches, covering a distance of about ten miles from Wentworth Hotel. The nearest, and one of the finest of the Rye Beaches, is called Wallis Sands; it is two miles distant. The whole of Rye, when it formed part of the territory of New Castle, was known as "Sandy Beach;" while the portion immediately adjacent, that is, along the southern and southwestern shore of Little Harbor, including the bordering lands of Seavey's and Sagamore creeks, was always described as "Little Harbor." There is no high land on the south. It is well wooded, and a fine country for walking and driving. It has an influx of several thousand visitors in summer; the permanent population is agricultural and inn-keeping. They live through the winter in the enjoyment of the past, and expectation of the next, season's harvest of summer boarders. They are very thrifty and great hoarders. In the war of the Rebellion they were about the only people in New Hampshire who had gold and silver money. It was said they drew it from long secreted stores, under their beds and in their cellars. This is probably an idle tale. Yet the custom of hiding money is still prevalent among country folk; it is singular, but they do not like to be thought rich. The robbers are not dead, you know; the tax gatherer is immortal, charity importunate, and neighbors envious. However, our neighbors on the south are said to be the richest, per capita, of any community in the State, and New Castle owes them a debt of gratitude for coöperating so generously in the building of a free bridge over Little Harbor into their domain.

The Wentworth towers are one hundred and seventy feet above the sea, and command, according to the mathematical formula of the U. S. Lighthouse Board for distances of objects from a given level, an horizon view of twenty-seven miles.

I have already described most of the objects in the foreground

view of the Wentworth towers. The life that animates the scene, one naturally looks for on the surrounding waters. There, on some days, everything is in motion; on others, the water is still as the earth and sky, and looks as if you might walk on its polished floor without miracle. Then the vessels seem to draw less water than among the waves; and those in ballast, with sails trimmed fore-and-aft, resemble a large fish, as he darts above the surface for a moment, with all his fins rigidly set. Now and then a fiery little steam-tug pushes across the harbor, wrinkling the sea on either side for a short distance, and leaving behind a long scribble of smoke in the tranquil and luminous air. Pleasure boats are becalmed, and must betake themselves to the ash breeze to get in to supper. Larger craft are waiting for the tide, that constant wind of the deep sea, to drift them to an anchoring ground. It is summer, but it is cool as well as calm. Perchance you are here for rest, for recovery from the weary year; then all is propitious, and you may regain the lost poise of the spirit, and health, in the salutary climate of New Castle.

But when the breeze springs up how the aspect of everything changes! Only at the seaside does one realize the power of wind; for there is his chief plaything, his victim, his slave, trembling or laughing at his lightest breath. There, the two elements, water and air, contend, and the earth is a witness and sometimes a sufferer. From the shore you see the battle, ever ending, ever renewed. You see the sails spread to profit by the struggle, or, to become the prey. The sea saith "I am not your enemy; go indict the wind." The wind saith "it is not in me; my might is without will; I obey your sail and your rudder, but a time comes when some other remorseless hand transforms me — I know not what I do!" Yet the brave vessels go forth prepared for the hazard; mere atoms between the two uncertain elements, but defying both. Surely, Capt. John Smith was right when he called a ship the noblest fabric of man.

The vessels most common in our waters are coasters, of various rig, two and three-masted schooners, sloops, fishing craft; and, in summer, yachts and excursion steamers; occasionally all the year round, foreign ships and our own men-of-war. These, with the small steamers that run to York and the Isles of Shoals, and different points up and down the river, the steam launches and small boats of the neighborhood, make up a pleasant and interesting scene. I like the blue, river street, which though wide is often crowded, but still noiseless. There is no heat, no dust, no mud, no shops. Occasionally I have seen as many as four hundred vessels becalmed and anchored between Whale's Back Light and the upper end of the harbor. At such times, when evening comes on, New Castle seems like the suburb of a great city. A thousand lights twinkle in long lines from mast and deck; dogs bark; you hear the chopping of wood, confused cries, singing and swearing, and you know by a faint smell wafted ashore, what the later comers are going to have for supper. And by the creaking of ropes in the blocks and the sound of oars you are conscious that it is a sea-city, a Venice moored here for a night, not a trace of which, perhaps, will be seen in the morning. A storm, a contrary wind, or a calm has brought them or left them here; but suddenly the wind comes out of the west, and they disappear as in a dream. In a stormy, dark night, with a head wind, you will hear some lone vessel's sail snapping as she comes about, trying to tack into port; then you offer up a prayer that she may not misstay.

Wentworth Hotel is in such a commanding situation that from its piazzas, and all its floors, the view of ocean and land is unobstructed. Within is every convenience known to the modern hotel. It is so many square yards of metropolitan comfort and luxury set on a seaside eminence, in the midst of a pleasant country. The grounds are well laid out in walks, terraces and flower plots; no attempt has been made to transform the natural character of the situation, but to adapt all improvements to it. The present owner is a lover of trees, and has planted a mile of elms on the road from the hotel to Sagamore bridge.

I have mentioned that the first hotel, about one-third part of the present, was built in 1874, by a gentleman who fell in love with the situation, but did not sit down to count the cost. In the year 1879, it fell into the hands of an owner who did not need to, and who has spared no expense to make it a perfect establishment, within and without. The good luck of New Castle is that it always attaches people, and both the owner and the present excellent landlord of the Wentworth, Mr. George F. Thompson, combine enthusiasm for the place, with due attention to business. The House contained originally eighty-two rooms, and cost about $50,000. The first addition was made in 1880; the second, in 1881;

by which the whole arrangement and architecture of the building were changed and improved. It now contains over two hundred rooms, and in consequence of their arrangement, and the natural advantage of situation, it can be said, without exaggeration, that every one of them has some pleasant view. And the same can be said of every other window in New Castle. The hotel faces southeast, so that the sun goes quite around it in summer, and this was the most ancient manner of setting a house on this island. If you find an old cellar hole here, you can tell infallibly where the front door was. The sun went around it in midsummer, leaving it in shade from noon to sunset, and in winter shining upon it all day.

The privilege of naming the Wentworth was granted to the present writer by the original projector, and was chosen on account of its proximity to the old Wentworth mansion, and its popular, widely-known associations; and also because the name itself is well-sounding, and, I dare say, slightly aristocratic; as much, however, I think, from its sound, as any immediate or general connection. At any rate it is a little superior to those names of hotels and of everything else, almost, in our country, chosen arbitrarily and multiplied indefinitely. Yet it has one weakness, it was borrowed. But what, since Adam's time, is not? We no longer invent names; we adopt and transfer, and it is fortunate if they prove to be appropriate.

The name of the hotel reminds us that a visit to the old Wentworth mansion was promised, and can be made from here in a few minutes, by water, or by a drive of two miles. The mansion is open to the public; fee, twenty-five cents. This fee has become necessary, for repair and protection of the council chamber, the best specimen of a colonial interior in this region, and also to guard its relics from the — absent-minded. The property should be owned and cared for by New Hampshire, for it is the most interesting monument of the colonial period in the State. It was built in 1750 by Gov. Benning Wentworth. It is necessary to be explicit in speaking of a Wentworth, for the family was numerous; and to be almost equally cautious about Wentworth governors, for there were three of them. Besides which, their inter-relations were much mixed; when they did not marry their cooks, they always appear to have taken their cousins and each other's widows. New Castle has the honor of having

not so easy to deliver it, and hardest of all, to collect the bill; and Samuel Allen died intestate, in New Castle, and lies buried somewhere inside the walls of Fort Constitution. Gov. Benning Wentworth managed it better. He fleeced the lamb but did not kill it; he took a portion from seven and from eight, but did not grasp at all, and followed the road of riches by steady accumulation. He was Governor of New Hampshire for a quarter of a century, and his term fell upon a time of great material and almost national developement in the eastern provinces. They were just learning to think, and, as a consequence, becoming self-conscious, and aware of a new order of things to be established on this continent. They were also learning the art of arms in their constant warfare with the Indians and French, which culminated in that mock-heroic expedition to Cape Breton and capture of Louisburg, to which I have already alluded. Gov. Benning Wentworth took an active part in the plans and preparations for this enterprise, and was the principal coadjutor of Governor Shirley of Massachusetts. He had an ambition to command the expedition; and was flattered by Governor Shirley with the confidential message that it would have been "an infinite satisfaction to me if your limbs would have permitted you to take the chief command." For Governor Wentworth had one aristocratic malady among the other proud and prosperous tokens of his exaltation, the gout. It was not, however, his stiff legs that lost him the command of the Louisburg expedition, but his stiff neck. He had no popular manners; he was respected, admired—at a distance; and the colony was satisfied now that it had, almost for the first time, after a long struggle, a Governor of its own, nominally, at least, independent of Massachusetts. So Governor Wentworth was permitted to remain in his mansion at Little Harbor, and enjoy himself after his customary manner, while Col. William Pepperell, of Kittery, led the yeomanry against the French. His selection is the most significant event in pre-revolutionary annals. A country store-keeper, justice of the peace and militia colonel; he was chosen in deference to the wishes of the men who had volunteered. It was a sign of the independence and growing power of the people, and an omen of what we were coming to, when popularity and any kind of success elevate men to military and political position, and Providence takes care of the result.

Governor Wentworth had a considerable share in the glory of the triumph at Louisburg, which astonished the world, and none more than the English government, which began from that time to be alarmed at the resources and power of the force it had itself called into activity. It confirmed the authority of Governor Wentworth in this province, which was undisturbed until the passage of the Stamp Act. He continued to increase in riches, and continually enlarged his style of living, adding new rooms and embellishments to his Little Harbor residence. Here he remained more and more, as his gout increased, and the traders of Portsmouth became more and more indifferent to royal insignia. His hospitality was great, but it was excessively formal and stately. Everyone was ambitious of an invitation to his dinners, and when he got there, yawned and wished it over. He held his councils in the great room of state, built for the express purpose; as the visitor will observe, on a lower level than the remainder of the mansion, for convenience of access from the water-side; and, also, probably to separate it more completely from the *res domesticæ*. Below the council chamber was stabling room for forty horses. Although the official meeting-place of the Provincial Councillors was in Portsmouth, on assembling they would usually find a summons from Governor Wentworth in this form: the Governor desires his respects, and invites the Council to his residence at Little Harbor, to drink the King's health. This meant business indeed, and consumed a long time; at the end of which, such as did not sleep under the table were provided with quarters among the fifty-two rooms of the mansion. It has now but forty-two. His will was supreme; the council but a form, and had plenty of leisure to discuss the merits of the Governor's wine and the new appointments he was always adding to his establishment, the last and most celebrated of which was Martha Hilton. The Governor was a man of extraordinary self-possession and firmness, but of narrow intellect. A long experience in following his own inclinations had made him arbitrary; and he could not brook opposition, especially in his personal concerns. He has become the hero of romance, but without one romantic trait. The state he kept colored the imagination of his contemporaries, as it has done that of posterity, and through it he himself is seen. When he ordered Rev. Arthur Brown, at the conclusion of a dinner party to marry him to Martha Hilton, he was supposed to have demeaned himself. But it was his great estate and office that people thought of, in this New Hampshire King Cophetua. There was nothing in the man superior to the beggar maid he had chosen. He himself was only two removes from an humble citizen of New Castle. But the Wentworths were all rather peculiar in their tastes about women. Once before had our present Governor Wentworth lowered his standard at the feet of a poor Portsmouth maiden, who rejected him for a shipwright. This slight, in due time, he requited, by abducting the innocent shipwright, and sending him on a cruise in one of his Majesty's war ships. But he was more lucky with Martha Hilton. She was handsome, and had the pride of her beauty; and she added to the gaiety and splendor of the Governor's establishment. Her family have protested that she was not as lowly born as is represented; her ancestors it seems were worthy fishmongers of London; but then, I do not find the name of the Wentworths in the Old Testament. It is time to have done with the claims and noise of descent, and that bastard of science, heredity, begot by astrology on evolution. Let us admit, once for all, that we are the sons of respectable grocers, with a few exceptions; the exceptions being the sons of haberdashers, and that we were born to serve Mammon and glorify the Ledger, which truly is the western synonym for that Book of Life so often mentioned in the sacred Scriptures. It has been objected to Longfellow's ballad of Lady Wentworth, as in his "Paul Revere's Ride," that he does not adhere to facts. Well, poets do not write history: they do something better, they imagine it. If it be a lie agreed upon, they make the lie agreeable and worth remembering; in fact, the only history that long survives. Was it not Gautier who said that what the poet invents, exists? But for this, faint will be the interest in Benning Wentworth, his doings, his mansion. Let us rejoice in his caprice in wedding a pretty servant girl, by which and the support of a ballad, his career and the time are lifted out of the dull, provincial procession of events.

The parlor and the council chamber are the only portions of the Wentworth mansion now shown to the public. The parlor is a fine old room, rather low studded, but on that account more comfortable looking; a room in which, with a cheerful, open fire, you might take your ease with your Martha Hilton, and defy the gossips. From the parlor you descend a short flight of stairs, through a quaint hall, in which are racks for muskets, and the great outer door of the council room. The council room is of good proportions and lofty. The wood-work of the fireplace is hand carved, and is said to have been a year's labor. Some good portraits adorn the walls; one by Copley of Dorothy Quincy, John Hancock's wife. There are also autograph letters of distinguished people, — Washington, Adams, and others. Several side rooms belong to it, for cards and billiards; and a beaufet for the wine and punch-bowl, never empty when the councillors were expected, — the Governor's prevailing argument in affairs of State. The situation of the Wentworth mansion is very retired, being a mile from any highway and reached by a road of its own. Little Harbor washes its walls, however, and this, in old times, was the more common way of going to it, as well as to all the other dwellings around the adjacent shores. It is still the most pleasant manner of approach. You see at once that they all, and especially the Wentworth mansion, were planted and constructed with reference to the water ways, and not the land.

Benning Wentworth was succeeded in office by his nephew, John Wentworth, the second Governor of that name. He expected to inherit his uncle's estates, but they all went to Martha Hilton (Lady Wentworth) who continued to reside at the Little Harbor seat, and married next Col. Michael Wentworth. Her daughter, by this husband, married Sir John Wentworth. Did I not say the Wentworths were much mixed? But we are not in pursuit of the family tree; three bulky volumes scarcely contain it. Sir John was the last Wentworth who occupied the mansion. I cannot say how it fared with Martha Hilton and her gouty Governor; but, as he was sixty and she twenty, we can guess. But when she married Col. Michael Wentworth she had more fun and less grandeur. They lived a life of pleasure, and contrived to spend the whole of the fortune left by the Governor. It was during this period that they entertained Washington, after his famous fishing excursion off New Castle. It was in 1789 that Washington made the tour of the Eastern States, and arrived in Portsmouth on the 31st of October. The next day being Sunday he went to church twice, two different sects dividing the honors. On Monday, November 2d, Washington went a fishing, with a

Mantle Old Wentworth House

band of music; in his diary he complains of his luck, and no wonder! The patriotic cod were all ready to be caught, but how could they find the hook in the din of a brass band? But a fisherman had provided against all chance, with a cod ready at the end of his line, which he handed to the Father of his Country. He draws him in, a shiny twelve-pounder, no poor-john, who gives a few gasps (while the band plays "Hail to the Chief") and expires, the most exalted codfish on record, not excepting that one who presides over the deliberations of the Massachusetts Legislature. I would he had been stuffed and mounted, to place among our New Castle antiquities; for he was of our own *gens Gadus*. As Washington passed Fort Constitution, on this excursion, he was saluted with thirteen guns. When the fishing was over, he was rowed up Little Harbor to the Wentworth mansion. It is not recorded that he stopped at Blunt's Island — that small point of land with one house upon it, just west of the free bridge — but there is no doubt that he did, that he must have, for here lived Capt. John Blunt, who was the pilot of his own boat in that famous Crossing of the Delaware. At the Wentworth mansion Washington was entertained in the grand style for which the house was celebrated. This was the last interesting scene associated with it. It was a fitting close to all we know of the career of Martha Hilton, that she should live to entertain the first President of the new republic — she who had been the wife of almost the last, and the most distinguished, of royal governors.

We cannot leave the Wentworth mansion without remarking the early and extensive connections of the family in this colony, and with all the prominent people of New Castle. The Sheafes, Jaffreys, Waltons, Atkinsons, Jacksons, and Frosts of this town were connected by marriage with the Wentworths. And, as has been heretofore alluded to, Samuel Wentworth, the oldest son of Elder William Wentworth, the founder of the family in this country, was an inhabitant of New Castle from 1669 to 1678; and during this period he kept a tavern, having "libertie to entertain strangers and to sell and brew beare, — at the sign of ye dolphin." At the time of naming our present Hotel Wentworth, I was unaware of this bit of local history; but now it seems a pleasing and surprising coincidence that the house should bear the name of the first recorded inn-keeper of New Castle. With the consent of the reader and the public, therefore, I hereby cancel my grounds for christening Wentworth Hotel, and do now declare it was in honor and memory of Samuel Wentworth, the earliest inn-keeper of New Castle. And hereafter the arms of Wentworth Hotel may most appropriately be a *Dolphin;* and let it be that swiftly-swimming, brilliantly-colored coryphene that carried Arion to Lesbos.

The ramifications of the Wentworth blood are endless, both in this country and England. Its annals are full of pictorial and literary material, which it is a wonder have not been more used. It was a race of no common anatomy. Among them, I remember a real Romeo and Juliet; a pair of nineteen-year-old and desperately unfortunate lovers, who divided a phial of poison, drank and died. Browning has indeed written into tragedy the history of one Wentworth, the Earl of Strafford; and that title, as well as another belonging to the family, Rockingham, are perpetuated in the names of two New Hampshire counties. The Wentworth genealogies have been compiled in three volumes by Hon. John Wentworth of Chicago, in the most minute manner, through all their windings. If anyone should suppose himself to be a thorough-going plebeian, let him hunt these books, and perhaps he will be as astonished as the writer of these pages, to find some maternal great-grandmother was a Wentworth, and that he has crept into the house by even a back door.

If you go to the Wentworth mansion by water, which is by far the more interesting way of approach, you can, after the visit, keep on and make a boat-excursion up Sagamore creek,

one of the ancient portions of New Castle. This creek can only be seen to advantage from a boat. Crossing it on a bridge is not seeing it. As before remarked, a creek is best taken with a good deal of water. Go up, then, on an afternoon or sunset tide, and stay for the ebb. You see then, and become a part of, the magical process by which a sea-creek is transformed and made beautiful or desolated, by the semi-diurnal impulse of the ocean stream. Life here has had, too, its flux and its ebb; not much is now left but memories. Families of renown originated here; their houses once studded the shores. I have spoken of the two movements of the families who made the first settlement on Odiorne's Point: one to New Castle, and up the shores of the Piscataqua; the other worked its way through forest and meadow to the head of Sagamore creek. The first was bent on trade, shipping and fishing; the other devoted itself to agriculture, and founded its homes among the good lands to the south and west of Mason Hall. Fully to appreciate the latter movement, the reader must not only explore Sagamore creek, but walk through the Strawberry Patch Road. This must be, I think, the oldest piece of highway in New Hampshire. It is now of use only to the few inhabitants left upon it. It runs nearly parallel and close to Sagamore creek; yet the creek is not seen from it until you reach the Langdon house. What I have to say of this region, therefore, must include and refer to both road and creek. Most of the dwellings were undoubtedly on the Strawberry Patch Road; but their lands extended to the creek, which was more often their means of intercourse with the neighborhood than the land ways. When New Castle was incorporated, in 1693, all this region was included in its bounds; and had become in ten years important enough to have always one of the three selectmen, and a constable of its own. The people went to church and paid tithes in New Castle; going across Little Harbor by ferry, or fording. Everything along the creek and Strawberry Patch Road has the flavor of the highest antiquity known in New England. Nearly every farmstead is on the site of the first; and the lands have never been alienated. Here are four thousand acres inherited from father to son for two hundred and fifty years. It is a region almost unique, in this respect, in all New England. One of these farms contains seven hundred acres, first occupied by Tobias Langdon, and now by his seventh descendant. Tobias Langdon had one child, of the same name, who was the father of "seven stately sons;" one of these was the ancestor of John Langdon, who was President of the first United States Senate, Governor of New Hampshire, and patriot of the Revolution. Here, also, was the cradle of the Lears and the Sherburnes.

The houses are all old and small; and many are gone. But the roadside is full of cellar-holes and family burial-places. The trees are venerable, and fine as can be seen anywhere. There are oaks, said to be survivors of the primeval forests. I take it that old customs remain here, too; for when the artist who made the accompanying sketches, was on the road with his pencil, last mid-winter, we saw, at the Tucker Farm, a burial going on beside a ledge in a lonesome field. And the yards and buildings indicate the old-fashioned style of farming. Many of those striking, un-Saxon names were once common here, as in other spots about the mouth of the Piscataqua. Those which belonged to the Sagamore creek region were Langdon, Sloper, Soper, Lear, Fowey, Bamfylde, Trefethen, Treworgy; add to these, Peveril, Pulsifer, Polkinghorne, Penhallow, and Champernowne, and I know of no more remarkable group of names in one small New England district. For much that is historically interesting about the Sagamore creek region, one needs a guide; but, sauntering there on a summer afternoon, memory and nature are enough. Going by boat we shall pass, on the right hand, the Martine cottage, almost hidden by trees. The lawn is washed by the creek; and to this, as to all the other dwellings we pass, it is evident the ancient approach was by water. Their road was the gift of nature. In 1798, Louis Philippe was a guest for some days at the Martine cottage; and flowers from its gardens were sent to him when he became King of France.

No place is without its local poet, or human oddity. As we go on we shall hear of several on these shores, in addition to which we call to mind a real hermit and a reputed witch, and at the head of the creek stand out the solid memories of the Langdons and Lears, of more universal fame.

The local annals of Sagamore creek mention Estwick Evans as a writer and traveller, and at all times eccentric. He flourished in the first half of this century, and would, perhaps, have

: Tucker Farm :

become considerable of an ornament to it, had not untimely love blighted his early ambitions. Thenceforth, he did unusual but not admirable things. He found it easier to be singular than to be great. He made a journey on foot to the Mississippi river, with a gun of his own height, two dogs, and clothed all in fur, from toe to crown. He proclaimed his object to be, to get nearer to a state of nature. Whether continual sermonizing was his ideal of a state of nature, I cannot say; but in the record of his travels there is endless moralizing and no tales, not even a fable. His book, called "A Pedestrious Tour," is one of the greatest curiosities of American literature. He was in Greece at the time of the revolution there; and finally settled down and died in Washington. His attachment to this creek continued to the end, and seems to have been the one bright and reasonable, though memorial thread in his life.

Just above the bridge — the only one over Sagamore creek — on the left bank, lived for eighty-two years the noted hermit, Benjamin Lear. I think he was rather left alone than chose to be. He was born while the farm of his family was still in the limits of New Castle. The Lears were long-lived; and Benjamin mightily feared old age would bring him poverty. He saved and saved, but in such small things that at last he became indeed poor. He spent his time in making his own clothes, doing his own housework, for the sake of economy, and neglecting his farm, until he had neither clothing, house nor farm. The land returned to wildness, his house decayed, his bed became straw, and he died one winter morning in two rags, one of which was his garment, the other his bed-covering. He had no interesting peculiarities, which sometimes compensate in such characters, the default of common sense. His seclusion made him an ancient before he became so in years; and he remembered and spoke of things as they were in his youth, and just as if there had been no changes since 1750. His memory lingers here on the shores of Sagamore creek, but there is not much reason for our lingering longer near his hermitage; only I cannot forbear to note that this man's mother had lived on the same farm as her hermit son for one hundred and two years, and toward the close of her long life she became much distressed by the fear that she should never die, and expressed her fears in almost the identical language of Mary Moody Emerson.* The spirit of the Wandering Jew seems to have entered into these two New England women; and to have been most ingeniously imagined in that gem of New England tales, "Peter Rugg."

In the middle distance of Sagamore creek the ledges on the left are high and bold, but trees clothe their summits; on the right, oaks grow so close to the shore that half their shade falls upon the water, and you can row under the branches and gather acorns, and the leaves, sacred to him who first taught mankind to eat the fruit of the oak and to fashion a drinking-bowl after the form of its cup. Here are several pretty miniature islands, with clean shores, and covered with young oaks, very islands of the blest, for peacefulness, rest and remoteness. The white oak that still grows around our shores and creeks, is celebrated among shipbuilders. Slow growing, it knits its fibre in a firmer and tougher ring than inland timber; and always acquainted with salt, either at the root or leaf, it absorbs a quality which preserves it longer from worms and decay. After this the creek broadens somewhat, and then narrows suddenly and soon loses itself in a marsh, beyond Lafayette road. In autumn, the marsh is ablaze with samphire weed. Where the creek begins to broaden, begin the lands of the old Langdon farm. Here are noble, open fields, sloping to the water. Let us row softly now, for we approach the tomb of a poet — John Elwyn. Under a solitary, ancient oak, at the foot of the field, washed every day by the tide, he lies buried, and realizes his last wish — which was that of Timon of Athens:

> "Timon hath made his everlasting mansion
> Upon the beached verge of the salt flood,
> Which once a day with his embossed froth
> The turbulent surge shall cover."

He was a true poet; for I call him a poet who has added one good line to his country's literature, and he wrote more than one. Alas, never to become the favorites of the fashionable poetical calendars for every day in the year, I fear. Yet, for one portion of our New England summer, June, he wrote the stanza which

---

* *See* Brewster's Rambles About Portsmouth, 2d Series, p. 207; and R. W. Emerson's Works, vol. x, p. 400.

comes nearer to the season itself than any I know. He is
unknown outside a little circle. He would not flatter his contemporaries, and scorned, or rather, never thought of the public
and popularity. He never published his writings, but printed
them and gave them away. This, among your regular book-
makers, will create an instant suspicion of want of sense in the
man, and want of value in his work; for have we not now, after
terrible struggles and the long odium of philistinism, brought
literature of all kinds, even poetry, where it must enter the market
like any other commodity? I trust so; and that we know, in this
advanced age, the worth of fiction and poems by the prices paid
for them. However, this was not John Elwyn's view, and he
was rich enough to indulge his foible. But hear a paragraph of
his last will and testament which, perhaps, is as good a key as
any to his temper. I must premise that he was the grandson of
Gov. John Langdon, and inherited his estates, and much else that
had come down through that family; one of the relics being the
old official seal of New Castle, which has been lately restored to
the town. The landed estate had never been alienated; and
when John Elwyn came into possession of it, he allowed not
even a tree in the seven hundred acres to be felled that had life
enough to stand. He made his nephew his heir, and requests
him not to sell any of the lands, and to live upon them; and
then adds the words which I wished to quote: "It is a good way
in the end this keeping of your father's lands; it roots you deep
in your own faith and where you rightest belong, and helps keep
you from the phantoms of the world; not that I mean any
idolatry of feudalism; though I hate the restless, predatory
spirit of this day and this nation." This was his manner in
prose; in verse he has more gaiety and abandon, yet is not lack-
ing in the most lofty imagination, and a style sometimes so close
to his thought as to produce the impression of genius. What a
delight it was to hear him recite old English lyrics! He delivered
them with all the emotion of one who had just written them.
He knew them all — by his heart. He knew the best in all litera-
tures, and had read, and continually, all the masterpieces in their
own tongues. He was reading the Hebrew Bible for the eleventh
time when he went to the company of the prophets and the poets,
for which he had so long and ardently prepared himself. His
"Transmigrator's Tale" is a poem of unequal but rare power·

and his memoir of John Langdon I have never yet read too many
times. The closing sentence of his will refers to his direction
that he should be buried where we are now looking— "in the
borders of his inheritance."

Here ends the beautiful part of Sagamore creek; and a little
way to the south, at the Langdon house, also ends the pleasant
Strawberry Patch Road. The Langdon house is not itself interesting, being one of those barn-like buildings so common in New
England country. Almost everybody's mother or grandmother
was born in one of them; that makes their interest; and we go
back to them and find them, actually or in memory, more dear than
the grandest houses. John Langdon left this homestead at
eighteen, and throughout his life saw and shared in all the great
events of his day. But this man, who was thought to be without
sentiment, and the most worldly-minded of all the Revolutionary
fathers, as he approached old age declined all office and honors, to
which he had only to give his consent to be elected; returned to
New Hampshire and gave himself up to meditation and religion.
The memory of his childhood, of his mother, filled his reveries;
and with his affecting and only confession of it, we will take
leave of the homestead to which it refers. What New England
country-boy has not played in the chips of the door-yard?
Seated on a wood-pile, with pole and line, we have fished
among those chips with as much fun and excitement as if they
were a pond full of pout and pickerel. But this is the way it
seemed to John Langdon in his old age; and I read it as the
epitome of the pious history of half of New England's sons:
"It is not affectation; my mind of itself turns to nothing but the
world I am hastening to, and the days of my childhood; it may
be the imbecility of age, but seventy years I have almost forgotten; the tall youth that left home with fifty dollars in his pocket,
the ocean on which he made his fortune, the Senate-rooms, the
counting-rooms and the ball-rooms, where he passed so much of
his life, are to me the history of a stranger; I hear my mother's
voice as I am playing at the door in the chips, of the house I
was born in; when by myself, I turn to the days of my childhood."

The earliest case of witchcraft recorded in New Hampshire
was in 1656, about thirty-four years before the appearance of
the "stone-throwing devil;" and it happened somewhere in the

Old Langdon Farmstead

vicinity of this creek, or at its junction with Little Harbor; it was, at any rate, within the territory of New Castle, so that both ends of the town could boast of their witches. I have already alluded to this case on page forty-six, as that of Susanna Trimmings. She was the complainant in the case; the witch was Goody Walford. It came to trial; but the witch was only bound over to respond at the next term of court, by which time the matter was suffered to disappear. Subsequently, Goody Walford turned the tables upon her prosecutors, and, much to the credit of this community, gained her cause against one of them in damages of five pounds — she had laid them at one thousand. The testimony in the first case, when Mrs. Susanna Trimmings was the accuser, is amusing. Susanna had a husband, Oliver, and one young child; their home was next by "the freshet." This, no doubt, would enable a skilful antiquarian to identify the spot; for the word means a small brook or pool of fresh water, and has rarely been used in that sense since the seventeenth century. Well, Susanna was going home one Sunday evening, by the said "freshet," and heard a rustling in the woods, which she thought might be pigs; but "presently after, there did appear to her a woman whom she apprehended to be old Goodwife Walford. She asked me where my consort was; I answered, I had none. She said, Thy consort is at home by this time. Lend me a pound of cotton. I told her I had but two pounds in the house, and I would not spare any to my mother. She said I had better have done it; that my sorrow was great already, and it should be greater — for I was going a great journey but should never come there. She then left me, and I was struck as with a clap of fire on the back, and she evanished toward the water side, in my apprehension in the shape of a cat." Then Mrs. Trimmings describes the dress of the witch, which must have been truly bewitching: "She had on her head a white linen hood, tied under her chin, and her waistcoat and pettycoat were red, with an old green apron and a black hat upon her head." Susanna took her oath to this before the three renowned fathers of the Province in those days: Bryan Pendleton, Henry Sherburne, and Renald Fernald.

Her husband, Oliver, testified that his dear Susanna got home in a sad state. "She sat down upon a chest and leaned upon her elbow." Three times he asked her how she did, but she answered not. Oliver was obliged to unlace most of her clothing and to pinch her, before she would speak. At length, she was able to relate her trouble, of which she became ill for some days.

Oliver testified that Goody Walford was at home at the time when she was said to be seen in red and green, asking for cotton,—a preposterous *alibi;* others, that it was nothing but Susanna's "fantasy." But John Puddington witnessed that Goody Walford "did *overlook* the cattle, which is as much as to say, in our country, *bewitching.*"

Puddington's wife deposed that she saw—a yellow cat! and that her John came and tried to shoot the cat; "cat got up on a tree, and the gun would not take fire and the cock would not stand." Afterwards she saw three cats—"the yellow one vanished away on the plain ground: she could not tell which way they went." Her John said it was a fact. Then comes the concluding witness with his innuendo, the meanest and chiefest of mischief-makers everywhere: They say they heard that Elizabeth told Nicholas she heard his Aunt Jane say she guessed, etc. In short, if you do not name Goody Walford, but declare you are sure there are just three witches hereabouts, "Thomas Turpin, who was drowned, Old Ham, and the third shall be nameless," you have fixed it upon poor Goody past all doubt. But honest Bryan, Henry and Renald couldn't see it clear, and adjourned for more light. It grew lighter, for the summer was advancing; the cats left off their pranks; Mrs. Susanna Trimmings presented her Oliver with a fine little Trimmings, got over her "fantasy," which Eliza Barton made bold to tell her was the only witch in the business,—and the neighborhood planted its corn and cured its fish, as usual.

INTERNAL ANNALS

RELIGIOUS AND CIVIL

"HONORABLE and worthy countrymen, let not the meanness of the word *fish* distaste you," said Capt. John Smith to John Bull, speaking of the commodities of these shores. That old adventurer knew little of freedom or religion; he looked upon this country much in the same manner as the modern citizen upon unopened fields, where his capital and enterprise may be employed profitably. In the same spirit the earliest settlers here, after a short period of indulgence in visions of mines of gold, precious stones, and other means of wealth without work, began to thrive on the near and actual resources of their situation. Fishing led to trade, both domestic and foreign, until the people became fixed in their occupations and interests, and moderately prosperous.

It was not until toward the close of the seventeenth century that the Province of New Hampshire began to be interested in matters of religious and political moment. It was then they, for the first time, felt the pressure of an authority in which they had no voice; it was then for the first time they heard that the prime object in the settlement of these shores was religious freedom. They were frightened by the knowledge of the former danger, and incredulous of the latter statement.

A preacher speaking, in 1691, on an ever popular theme (the depravity of the age) thus alluded to this point: "You have forsaken the pious habits of your forefathers, who left the ease and comfort which they possessed in their native land, and came to this howling wilderness to enjoy without molestation the exercise of their pure principles of religion." "Sir," interrupted one of his hearers, "Sir, you are entirely mistaken in the matter; our ancestors did not come here on account of their religion, but to fish and trade." The objector was undoubtedly correct; yet, the community having become established, one of its first needs was a church. The forefathers of New Hampshire may have been traders and fishermen, but they were just as pious as other folks. They had, however, bad luck; they were attached to the English church, and tolerated some of its clerical representatives, who proved to be unworthy shepherds; and this was made an article of wrath against them by the Massachusetts Bay Puritans. Then schismatics of all sorts overran the Province; it was their hunting-ground; and, first and last, there have been more strange speculations in religious matters in New Hampshire than in any other New England State. This has been, no doubt, in consequence of the primitive conditions, — the freedom of opinion, the absence of Puritan restrictions. I believe that Portsmouth was one of the first places where Universalism found a foothold; and once it had a Sandemanian church; and Unitarianism appeared there almost as soon as anywhere. And in Hampton I have discovered the first, the great original, Transcendentalist. Perhaps he is known to others; but a discovery, made independently, is good for the hundredth time. The Rev. Henry Allein believed emphatically in pure spirit; Adam and Eve more naked than we picture them, not even clothed with flesh; all is an emanation, all is soul; we do not rise from the dead — we never, in fact, have died — and it is more than doubtful if we have any bodies. All is a purely spiritual process; nothing is literal or real; Arthur and Fidelia are merely figures of speech. The ordinances of the Gospel are matters of indifference; only that which is spiritual, incapable of form, is of any value; it cannot be interpreted; it fits you like the surrounding air, but cannot be worn like a garment.

But why should I go as far as Portsmouth and Hampton for local theologic novelties? Voltaire said England was a country with one soup and fifty religions. New Castle has never invented a soup, but she has added one religion to the fifty.

Its rank in the hierarchy is not high, but it is a respectable sect of most worthy people and ministers, and deserves the thanks of mankind for some service in shattering the monstrous doctrines of Calvin. It has no abstract name, but is known as the faith of the Free Will Baptists, and was first preached by Benjamin Randall, who was born here in 1749. His first followers were called by various names: Randallites, General Provisioners, New Lights, Freewillers, and, in 1799, authoritatively, Free Will Baptists. Randall was a serious-minded person in his youth, and of beautiful character. Being converted under the preaching of Whitefield, he joined the Congregational church in New Castle; which always, on that account, has claimed him and his work as its child and a part of its history. He began to announce his peculiar views about 1780, and they spread throughout New Hampshire and Maine. I will not undertake to state what his disciples believed; it was another protest —

—"I know they a'l went
For a general union of total dissent."

They looked toward a return of primitive Christianity. In practice, the Free Will Baptist church is among the more liberal. Its ministers often carry on farming, or labor at some trade; and this is in accordance with a theory of the sect, that its clergy should not be set apart strictly, nor be highly educated. Yet, wherever, in Maine or New Hampshire, you find a Free Will Baptist society, you are almost sure to find uncommon intelligence, and a friendly and cheerful people. They have shaken off the black cloak of Geneva.

The Free Will Baptist church of New Castle was organized about 1787; it divided the town with the old Congregational church. Its first report to the other churches of the same persuasion was made in 1787 by a woman, Abigail Amazeen.

Benjamin Randall was the son of a sea-captain of the same name. This is an old New Castle family name. One of the first selectmen, in 1693, was James Rendel. He received what was called in those days a mercantile education. His trade was that of a sail-maker, and when twenty-one years of age, he began business for himself in New Castle. At about the same time he married Joanna Oram; and himself and wife, in 1772, joined the Congregational church of New Castle. In the Revolutionary war he was an orderly sergeant in the regiment of Col. Hercules Mooney.

While holding social religious meetings in the houses of some brethren who had become dissatisfied, like himself, with the New Castle church, he suddenly threw down the volume of sermons from which he was reading and confessed his conviction that he must become a preacher. This was the beginning of trouble for him. New Castle was used to an educated clergy; should a sail-maker presume upon the sacred function? and heresies to boot? Have we not known this little, hazle-eyed, sharp-nosed Benjamin all our lives — and *he* wants to be a great man, a preacher! Let him stick to his palm,* his sail-loft, and his Joanna. In short, he came very near being persecuted, which only made him more stubborn in his determination, and led him to cutting remarks, in which he was uncommonly gifted. Bricks were thrown at him, and language, not too choice; but nothing could hurt him. Tar and feathers were prepared as he should go by a certain gate; but he took another. He was informed that a company of forty men were banded to mob him; "Ah," said Randall, "that is the Devil's old regiment; he once raised forty men to kill brother Paul. He missed it; he will now. God calls; I must go." He went to his preaching; by its power, a heavy thunder-storm coöperating, the mob was dispersed and got a good ducking.

In the end Randall was triumphant; his fame was great, both here and in the surrounding towns. In one spring, 1777, thirty were converted and baptized. It was said New Castle had never seen such days before; it has often since. Before, it had been sufficient to be sprinkled in your long clothes, to have a pew and pay tithes when you were old enough, to listen to an educated ministry and to have a creed. Randall believed in none of these things; he would earn his bread like other men, and he continued his trade of making sails while here, and when he removed inland, changed his palm for a thimble and became a tailor. He worked in the night that he might preach by day; he went wherever he was called, or where "impression" — this was his modest word for divine direction — led him, and seldom spoke less than three hundred times in the year. I do him and his sect some injustice when I use the words preach, sermon, minister or church. To them these terms smacked of an hireling church. Everything must be voluntary with them; it was the spirit, not Harvard College, that fitted a man to help his fellows; and preaching they called "improvement;" for example: "Next

---

* Sail-makers' term for a shield of leather worn on the palm of the hand.

evening, likewise, I *improved* again at the same place." Their creed was the New Testament at large, neither reduced nor selected. The old articles of his church in New Castle are utterly simple, mainly about its polity; three in number, and short, and in the year of our Lord 1844, were condensed to one. Reader, couldst not thou and I belong to such a church? Here was one more brave attempt to unite men in a simple faith; but, alas, it began and goes on, as usual, by division. It nearly ruined the old church, and the new struggles for life. Yet they live and will continue to live; for no community is so small as not to be divided on religious questions; and antagonism and pride are usually sufficient to keep open at least two churches, each with half a congregation and half a mite for the preacher. But there is no doubt that the sincerity and power of Benjamin Randall moved New Castle to a higher plane of religious life. He preached, *i. e.* "improved," constantly, either in the school-house or private houses. Church there was not as yet; nor am I able to find when one was first built. As to the usual properties of religious sects, the Free Will Baptists had few; and they believed in few. Water they had in abundance, and it was their chief convenience here, and their all-important symbol. One of Randall's successors, Elder Mark Fernald, could boast that he had been baptized in the Atlantic Ocean. Here was no shallow stream, or muddy mill-pond, which, as once happened to Randall while he was leading a company of converts to be baptized, might be drawn off by a member of an opposing church. And there was something sublime in the thought that nothing less than an ocean was commensurate with the infinite stain of mortal life; and here, at the very doors of the sinner, it came and invited him to wash and be clean. It was a powerful persuasion; it appealed to a people set in the midst of the seas, with a singular and natural force; and sailors and fishermen became acquainted with the element of their vocation in a manner to lend it a new and solemn character.

But ever woman is the larger and more enduring factor in all new religions. The emotions are the foundation of her being, and the spring of piety, of novel and vital religions. Man comes with his understanding, his scheme or his creed, and by that time faith is gone. Randall professed no creed; but, though he stood erect, used few gestures, and had not a loud voice, he never preached without tears in his eyes. This touched the feminine heart, and it founded his church in a sure place. Its outward existence mattered not; it might lose what the old elders significantly called its " visibility," yet, all the same, it could not die. Many women were baptized, both old and young, but more young. It was the outward token of conversion; but even that was not insisted upon; it was left largely to the choice of the individual. A lovely young woman who had become religious, yet had refused to be baptized, being filled with remorse, went alone into the sea, and in the attempt to baptize herself was drowned. Is not that a pathetic scene, when you think of it?

A woman made the first report from this church; and at its reorganization in 1827, which is the earliest date of the existing book-records, " four men and seven sisters" signed its three articles. One of those sisters now lives, a venerable woman ninety-three years old, who told me but yesterday, in the most unaffected manner, that she had lived enough, that she wanted to get to heaven, for which place she set out fifty-seven years ago. Under the preaching of two women, Nancy Towle and Clarissa H. Danforth, this church had two remarkable revivals.*

But there came another wave of religious reformation, which swept many of the Free Will Baptist churches from their old connection, and the New Castle church changed its name at least, if not its belief. In 1844, November 11th, it dropped the name of Baptist and assumed the name of the Free Christian Society; and, as I have already noted, dropped at the same time, two of its three former articles of agreement. The sect with which it now affiliates is sometimes called, but incorrectly, Christian Baptist; another mistake in the name is Christ-ians. They are

---

*Miss Nancy Towle wrote a singular book entitled " Vicissitudes Illustrated." A second edition was printed in Portsmouth, N. H., 1833. The preface was by Lorenzo Dow. Its grammar is entirely original; not at all in the sense of illiterate, but, so to speak, hyper-grammatical—such stilts as English never walked on before in these parts. The subject-matter of the book is mainly her travels, experiences and labors; scripture, anecdotes, family matters, warnings, dreams and dresses are mingled in a truly feminine fashion. She is very nice about words — puts a dash between the initial and final letters of those she thinks naughty.

" Hire grettest ooth nas but by seynt Loy."

Her book contains the first printed account of a visit to the Mormons, and an interview with Smith, which is of high value, being very circumstantial.

neither one nor the other, but simply what we all claim to be, Christians. They fraternize more with the Free Will Baptists than with other denominations; perhaps on account of their former connection, for they were all outgrowths of the Free Will Baptist churches, and I cannot see much difference in their belief or practice.

Out of the old protest against Calvanism made by Randall and his disciples, sprang many strange, grotesque varieties of belief. His immediate followers, however, were nearly all simple, sincere men, with a genuine apostolic spirit. His first active coadjutor was a New Castle man, John Trefethen. They travelled into the remote borders of this State and of Maine, crying in every wilderness. Their business was revivals. They saw no other path to heaven than through fire and water. Their work never was done, and always needed doing over. So they exhorted and prayed continually. But not in long sermons, or immoderate prayers. They were often strikingly brief and pointed. Here is a specimen of one of their prayers, good enough for a ritual : " O Lord, teach us each to feel the need of thy grace, and seek it; to know thy will, and do it; to find our place, and keep it. Amen." They reproved each other's faults in the boldest manner, by an open vote often. At a certain meeting, " it was voted that N —— M —— be admonished for anger, peevishness and swapping horses." This was a relic of Puritan discipline.

The ministers of the Christian church, which succeeded the Free Will Baptist in New Castle, were all the same stamp of men. One of them, Elder Mark Fernald, lived in Kittery, but preached here as much as anywhere. He was descended from a brother of Renald Fernald, the first surgeon of Great Island, among the earliest emigrants here. Elder Mark was a sailor and carpenter when not exhorting, at which he had a great gift. He was a quaint, witty speaker. He first made his hearers laugh, but soon brought them to their knees. His voice could be heard a mile in prayer — so he says — and I know not how many in sermon. Perhaps distressed sailors could hear it; at any rate he believed the Ruler of the tempest could; and no storm raged that did not find him on his knees throughout the dangerous darkness, offering the prayer of the boatmen of the Finistere, " Pity us, O God, for our boat is so little, and your sea is so big." Sometimes he was in a boat himself, giving practical help.

These are the saints of the dissenting churches. There was no measure in their readiness for self-sacrifice; they effaced every worldly ambition from their hearts, and took the vow of poverty. "I beg my bread barefoot to heaven," said Randall. They all had some trade or common labor. Elder Fernald was as often the physician of bodies as of souls; and, in general, they all served their neighbors and their followers in every benevolent, humble office. The same charge was made against them as the first opponent of Christianity, Celsus, made against the early ministers: "Wool-workers, cobblers, leather-dressers, the most illiterate and vulgar of mankind." Randall and his band were not learned or literary, and I do not know of any printed sermons left by them. But there are other writings, letters, journals, etc. There is extant a letter of Elder Mark Fernald to his only child, a daughter, on the occasion of her leaving home to learn, in Portsmouth, the trade of a tailoress. For beautiful simplicity of language, directness, and that wise counsel which comes from the depths of the heart, it cannot be easily equalled.

Friendly reader, you will never be able to reward me for the infinitely dreary and obscure waste through which I, as a faithful chronicler, have to dig my path in this little history. But occasionally I find such a long hidden beam of light, like the one just mentioned, such an almost literary master-piece, that I am content, and begin to believe, what I have half suspected before, that some of the treasures of New England intellectual and spiritual life, are quite unknown to the reading public.

New Castle has good reason to be proud of Benjamin Randall and the work he accomplished; and of Joanna Oram, his wife, who was faithful to the end, sharing all his labors, trials and poverty. He always spoke of her as the gift of God to him. Randall lived and preached, the latter part of his life, in New Durham. He was also the tailor of the town; and tried, meanwhile, to fashion for himself a heavenly robe. There is not the smallest doubt that he succeeded. He was all but worshipped by his followers. His labors by day and night, his travels in all weathers and seasons, his intense love for the souls of men, those tears so costly for him and so precious to his disciples, wore him out prematurely. His monument is in New Durham, but New Castle claims his name. His house, now gone, was in one of the most romantic nooks of the island, a little south of the scene of the "stone-throwing devil's" performances.

Randall's movement drew after it a number of impostures, as the Cochranites and Angelites; and others without name, represented by some visionary individuals who proclaimed their whims as a new dispensation. One man — I rescue his name from oblivion unwillingly — Elliot Frost, announced that he should never die. It was a bold stand to take among mortals; but he did live so long, both himself and his boast were forgotten. The same man, just before the great fire in Portsmouth in 1802, went through the streets prophesying, in a loud voice, death and destruction; and it was remembered afterward, that wherever he walked the fire followed, and that wherever he sat down and left off crying, there the fire stopped. His most singular performance was going naked through a neighboring town; this was meant to symbolize to the people their spiritual nakedness. He had one follower in New Castle, a woman, who, in the garb of her mother Eve, walked into church during the service. The preacher broke off his sermon and began to shout and sing in such a manner that the attention of the audience was concentrated upon him, and hardly anyone saw her save himself.

There was great freedom of speech in the Free Will Baptist and Christian congregations. The elder who stood in the desk was liable to be sharply catechised; and you might expect to be prayed for by name; to hear your short-comings and weaknesses mourned for. But then, you could retaliate in kind, provided you had kept sharp watch of the brethren and sisters during the week. Though they suffered much obloquy in the community, they complained of but one thing, namely, paying tithes to the established church. In 1819, the Toleration Act of New Hampshire removed this grievance; and, though I have been unable to find the exact date, I believe it was about this time that the Free Will Baptists built themselves a small house of worship. In 1845, just after changing their style to Christian, they removed their house, which stood a little west of its present position and close to the street, and remodelled it. Elder Boothby was then their preacher, and the society was very prosperous. Since 1845, it has had various fortunes; or misfortunes. For, in most small New England towns, the churches struggle for existence. Religion has become too expensive for poor men. I am sure that is why they no more go to church: they cannot afford it, and their honorable pride prevents their attendance as long as they are unable to contribute to the expenses. And there is something ignominious in a free church for the poor, while there are those not free. Randall was essentially right; no man should preach who is not first willing to do it without pay; and an expensive church is one more luxury for the rich, one more burden for the poor.

When you draw three sectarian lines through a total population of six hundred, the share falling to each must be minute; and when you count the cost of a separate organization for each, it is clear one or the other, and generally all three, are more or less embarrassed.

The first division in New Castle befell in the Congregational church. The second took place mainly in the body whose annals I have been recounting, and grew out of a belief in the predicted end of the earth. A few disciples gathered themselves together on this speculation and built a small chapel, where they continue to hold meetings, in spite of the failure — shall I say of their hopes or their fears? Several times they, and believers from adjacent towns, have assembled in New Castle, as a good point from which to see the " Coming of the Lord," and take their departure with Him. It is indeed: New Hampshire began here, why should it not end here? Although, in my younger and classical days, I was used to compare New Castle with the Peiraeus, to which it bears a remarkable resemblance, in situation, size and shape, I am now rather of the opinion that it may be the modern Patmos, on account of the visions which our Johns, not only see, but expect to behold realized from this island. Dwellers on hills and plains may look, naturally, in the clouds for the fifth act of our earth's drama; but here we expect it, instinctively and appropriately, from whence come all signs and wonders, the sea. We have frequent miniature rehearsals, as it were, of the final catastrophe, when the equinoctial north-easter arrives on our coast — when the foundations of the deep are broken up and the shoreland looks one black chaos. When your twelve-foot square chimney begins to rock, there are reasonable grounds of anxiety for the event. Nothing carries you calmly through it but long-established confidence in the geology of New Hampshire and much experience of the failure of prophecies. Until the Farmer's Almanac — our dear old Leavitt's — gives us due warning, we shall continue to sow, and, perhaps, reap. Yet, undaunted by the mis-calculation of their arithmetic since 1843, our Adventist friends go on ciphering. I surmise the difficulty is — too many ciphers. 'Tis a long account since Daniel, and I fear much of it is outlawed. We must begin again. Here is to-day; let us begin with it. Yet, they say, it is better to be prepared for the worst. It is wonderful how sensible and interesting men and women are six days out of the week. On the seventh, beware of them; it is a holiday in their brains, also. Yet this reaching after something, we know not what; this reference to some great mystery — one thing on which we cannot lay our hands — that is never alluded to in any popular newspaper nor in few books, this weekly respite from labor, from cheating and hoarding, whether it call itself Adventism or Millenarian or Muggletonian, is by far the most interesting and curious phase of village and rural life in New England, because the only time and the only themes on which the people entirely abandon themselves. Hear your neighbor arise in meeting and exhort or supplicate; can you believe him the same man with whom you spent the whole of yesterday and heard no syllable or suggestion of anything higher than his hands and eyes? Is it clear which is the real man? At any rate it throws over him an impenetrable mystery, and well might make you revise your opinion of the whole of mankind.

Among the people who have broken away from the older churches and organized various small societies, the smallest difference in opinion proves to be fundamental, and is enough to set up another church upon. Thus the Adventists of New Castle, though when all combined, too few to support a preacher, are now widely divided in matters of belief. Every new itinerant has his whim, and it obtains credit with some. The last new light was the necessity of baptism three times, the candidate kneeling all the while in the water; and, strangest of all, was the notion that it was wrong to offer prayer in the presence of the unconverted. I speak of these things not lightly, but to show how our New England village communities are preyed upon by imposters, self-deluded perhaps, in the guise of religion. These, with the glib book-agent and his worthless wares, now a Bible all shammiest of gilt, print, picture and paper; or the humorists' bibles for vulgarizing every sentiment and association; or a twelve-dollar county history with its local flatteries, concocted and published in some distant city; these, and every sort of peddler of cheap frauds, do more to impoverish communities of humble working-men than all the natural accidents and misfortunes of their lives.

The Adventist brethren who have assembled here from other parts to await the day of doom, had to be fed and lodged. One poor, but too hospitable brother, was heard to remark that if the world didn't end soon he should be a ruined man! And it is reported that the leaders and great prophets of this faith have taken much money from the town. Of course it is rather easy to borrow and beg of men who honestly believe they shall have little further need of their property. The Anglo Saxons sometimes borrowed money to be repaid in the next world; this ancient custom appears to have been revived in New Castle in the nineteenth century. God forbid that we should meet our creditors and debtors hereafter, whatever else may be met! But when simple men begin to speculate in religion, there is no knowing what will happen. They may legislate God out of existence, as once in Paris; or, legislate Him in, as Catholic and Puritan have attempted; or, as I have narrated in the preceding pages, be led into an unarticled, yet beautiful faith, declining at length to mere vagaries and individualism. The remedy is in greater intelligence. Our children will be wiser and better than we.

I have now cleared the way for some account of the older church in New Castle; and I have followed this irregular order, putting the most recent church first, because the history of the older is closely connected with the second and final portion of my subject; that is, the civil annals of the town. Everyone knows the intimate relation of church and town, in the early history of New England. In New Hampshire, this connection continued into the first quarter of the present century. The fundamental reason for town organization was that there might be a church; that it might have a legal standing; that taxes might be levied, and a tithe appropriated for the support of a minister and other expenses of a religious establishment. When, therefore, the people here asked to be incorporated as a town, the chief ground of their petition was that they might have a church of their own. Now this does not, by any means, signify that they had none; it means that they wanted authority to tax the whole community for its support, and have a "settled ministry;" a business upon which they would not enter until assured of the right to exact contributions from all citizens according to their property.*

I am particular in thus stating the situation in New Castle, because it has been often asserted, and quite naturally inferred from the language of the several petitions for incorporation, all of which dwell upon the fact of the difficulties of getting to Portsmouth to meeting, that there was no church building and no religious services here prior to the beginning of the eighteenth century. And the common statement is that Rev. John Emerson was the first settled minister in New Castle, of the date 1703. All printed references give this date as well settled. Our oldest town records, recently discovered, begin in 1693, and reveal new and important facts concerning the New Castle church; and prove conclusively that there had been settled ministers before John Emerson. These facts were unknown when the tablet to the memory of the pastors of the church was put up, for it begins with the name of Emerson. But before Emerson had been Rev. Samuel Moody.

Here permit me to introduce some documentary evidence, with which my readers cannot accuse me of having encumbered my narrative hitherto. It is, however, time for a more severe style, and that we make an offering to Clio, the muse of history. Until this present writing she has never been allowed to smile since the days of Herodotus; and was like to become the stiffest and leanest old maid of the sacred nine; always either too grandiose or too prim. But we have implored her to unbend; we never allow her to pass by any good story. Now, however, she shall resume her book and her Sunday manners.

On October 29th, 1694, according to our town records, this vote was passed: "Then ordered that ye town shall choose and call a minister themselves." Several public meetings were called

---

* A relic of this ancient custom still continues in the Unitarian church at Portsmouth; the regular members of which are assessed according to the city valuation of their estates.

to consider this business; and it is evident, from the stately formality and precision of the orders passed, that the town felt it was entering upon a very solemn enterprise. At length they approached a decisive point; they appointed a committee to "discourse" Mr. Samuel Moody. A special meeting was summoned to hear their report, which was that the committee had agreed with Mr. Moody for seventy pounds (in money) per year; he finding himself "housing and all other conveniences at his own charge." This report was signed by Robert Elliot, Elias Stileman and Shadrach Walton. It was ratified by the meeting after the following manner: " Read the above return at this general town meeting and put it to vote; it is consented to and agreed upon that acced. to ye above agreement made by Mr. Robt. Elliot, Maj. Elias Stileman and Capt. Shadrach Walton, the town will pay Mr. Sam. Moody seventy pounds each year he stayeth here settled minister, and that his answer is satisfactory to the town — and is settled minister for this town during his abode here in the ministry." Somewhat tautological, truly, is the style of Francis Tucker, our honorable town clerk for 1694; but it was new business and he had not got his hand in. Evidently the glory of a new town, and the dignity of a settled ministry, were too much for his quill. The evidence, however, is what has an important bearing; it proves a settled ministry in one year after the incorporation of the town; and Mr. Moody continued in it nine years, or until 1703, the date of Mr. Emerson's settlement. This I find shown by the record, that in 1703 Mr. Moody began to complain of arrears of salary. The town voted to pay him the debt in money; and, in future, part money and part provisions. But it is possible Mr. Moody did not accept this compromise, or actual reduction of his stipend, as his labors here came to an end in the same year.

It may be useful to put on record the few known facts concerning Rev. Samuel Moody. He was the son of Rev. Joshua Moody; was graduated at Harvard College in 1689, in the same class with John Emerson, his immediate successor in the New Castle church. After leaving here he preached at the Isles of Shoals, and then entered the army as an Indian fighter, a taste for which he had perhaps imbibed while in New Castle, from his friends, Maj. Stileman and Capt. Walton, both of whom were famous soldiers in their day, and chief men of Fort William and

Mary. Moody became a major in the king's colonial forces, and was stationed in New Foundland, Casco, and finally Falmouth (now Portland) where he died in 1729. Two sons were born to him while he was minister of the New Castle church, Joshua and Samuel; the former graduated at Harvard College in 1716; the latter in 1718, in the same class with Theodore Atkinson, a native of New Castle.

I have now shown that there was a settled minister in New Castle nine years before Emerson's time. There are other documents to show a much earlier date for this church. The minutes of the General Association of New Hampshire (Congregational) give the date of 1671 for the organization of a church in New Castle. I do not know the source of their authority. The date is probably confounded with that of Portsmouth. But there are proofs in our oldest town records of a church long before 1671. Here is a significant extract, from the record of the first town-meeting under the charter; the date is the 20th December, 1693: It was called to be held "in ye *meeting-house*; to agree with a minister and discourse other things necessary for the town's benefit." There was, then, a meeting-house in 1693; in 1694 a vote was passed ordering "a gallery to be made in the lattermost end of ye meeting-house for the women to sit in." This confirms the fact of its existence. But the evidence of its age is shown by the record of the year 1704, in regard to a new one. Theodore Atkinson, the first of that name in New Castle, was, by a vote of the town, "employed in getting the meeting-house now framed, or near framed, raised, enclosed, floored, with the pulpit and doors, and glazed, shingled and clapboarded." And August 22d, 1706, "voted, that Mr. Joseph Simpson lay out 50s in glazing ye new meeting-house, being so much money due to ye town from said Simpson for *ye frame of ye old meeting-house* and what boards was to it." There was then a church building at the time of the incorporation of the town, 1693, already so old as to require at that date repairs, and soon after was given up and sold for 50s, and a new one built. But we can follow, by help of the records, and the book called "Lithobolia," from which I have previously quoted in the account of the "stone-throwing devil," the line of New Castle clergymen, as far back as 1682.

Rev. Benjamin Woodbridge is cited in "Lithobolia" as a witness to the events narrated in that book. Now, as he was preaching here, according to our town records, from December, 1693, to October, 1694, and on the latter date his advice was asked by the town in the choice of a new minister, it is probable that he was here at least from the date of the " stone-throwing devil," 1682, to the settlement of Mr. Moody in 1696.*

Farther back than 1682 there is nothing but tradition to follow. This speaks of a Rev. Robert Jourdan as a minister here, in the earliest settlement of the island. He was born in England, and educated for the Episcopal church. The first notice of him in this country is in 1640, at Cape Elizabeth, Me. Very soon after that he removed to New Castle, where he died, between January and July, 1679. One of his sons married a daughter of Elias Stileman, captain of the fort. Such are the few known facts; from which the presumption is that he was the incumbent of the New Castle church at its foundation, and continued as long as it was suffered to remain under Episcopal forms. The obscurity concerning him may be due to natural circumstances; but as the Puritan hand is seen in the certificate of his mercenary character, it is likely his memory, in connection with this church, was suppressed. The ledge on which Walbach Tower stands was known as Jourdan's Rocks; and near by, in the enclosure of Fort Constitution, was his house, and there he was buried, as well as many others of the early inhabitants of New Castle. The name of Robert Jourdan appears among the petitioners for a town charter; and he was, no doubt, a descendant of the Rev. Robert Jourdan. The family became extinct in New Castle in the beginning of the present century; the last member of it was the widow of Nathaniel Jourdan.

But though it is not, at present, possible to fix the dates in the history of the New Castle church prior to about 1680, the fact of an ancient meeting-house in 1693, so old as to make a new one necessary, permits us to conjecture that it was built as soon as the place had a small population; that is, between 1630 and 1640. And the natural explanation of the language of the various petitions for a township, which all affirm the difficulties of

---

* This Benjamin Woodbridge is of a little interest, as the nephew of that minister, of the same name, who heads the list of the first class of Harvard College, in 1642.

attending meeting in Portsmouth and the desire for a church of their own, is this: the early settlers in New Castle were of the English church; as soon as they were able they built a house of worship, and had such clergymen as could be obtained from time to time, of their own faith. This, I may say in passing, was the situation in general, in the beginning of this Province; and there were several Church of England clergymen here, whose history is well known.

Then, from various causes, chiefly the authority and power of the Massachusetts Bay colonists, to whom this Province early submitted, the forms of faith became changed; and where they did not, the English church service became difficult to hold, if not dangerous. The Puritans became dominant in Portsmouth and established a church there. Portsmouth also began to increase in population; trade, which formerly centered at New Castle, moved up the river, finding Portsmouth a more convenient situation; and, though New Castle remained the seat of the civil, and the stronghold of the military, power, she gradually lost her importance and the church declined. Its pulpit was occupied irregularly. Very likely the religious sympathies of the people grew more and more in harmony with those of the Massachusetts colonists, as it is certain their political opinions did. When there was no minister in New Castle, the people went to the Portsmouth church; but this led, on account of the distance and effort required to get there, to considerable laxity in morals and religion. Moreover, they began to be taxed for the support of the Portsmouth church, for something of which they did not receive the full benefit, and which they preferred to pay at home, as they had been accustomed to do, though, as I have said, irregularly, and probably voluntarily. This is very clear, by the documents of the second volume of the New Hampshire Provincial Papers, where we read that when the Provincial Council called upon the Portsmouth selectmen to appear before them to answer the petition of the inhabitants of Great Island for a township, the Council asked them by what right they had assessed a tax on the citizens of said island. The whole implication of the documents is that there was no such right, and that it was a new thing. And this attempt to assess Great Island was a primary, moving cause of the request to be made into a separate town; which, being granted, no other change took place in the religious affairs of the island than the regular settlement of a minister at a fixed salary, to be raised by legal assessment. Throughout the whole period covered by the petitions, some ten or twelve years (from 1682 to 1693) there was not only a minister here, but a church, whose history it is at present impossible to trace clearly, yet whose age in 1693, so great as to require repairs and soon after pulling down and building anew, is a vivid evidence of the antiquity of New Castle. The truth is, there is a period in its affairs of about one generation, from 1650 to 1693, when its history is too obscure to be accurately followed; but, to some extent, may be fairly inferred.

I have now given a cautious outline of it, so far as it concerns the history of the church.

The first church building stood near to what is now the outer entrance of Fort Constitution.* All the early dwellings were grouped about the fort; but all traces of them have been obliterated long since, by the enlargements, from age to age, of the fort and its enclosures.

I shall now sketch briefly the remaining annals of the Congregational church. On the 24th May, 1703, Rev. John Emerson was invited by the town to become its minister, at a salary of £65, " besides the contributions of strangers." The town also promised to build a parsonage, but put it off from time to time. During Mr. Emerson's ministry, however, a new church was completed. Its site was directly in front of the present building. Mr. Emerson often reminded the people of their promise to build him a parsonage; many town-meetings were called to consider the matter, always ending in a vote to build; but votes did not then suffice to begin it even; at last, Mr. Emerson finding his house too inconvenient and his salary too small, called the people together and informed them that he found the " ayre " not agreeable to his " thin constitution," and that it would be absolutely necessary for him to move farther away from the sea. Accordingly, he removed to that distant, inland town, Portsmouth! While settled in New Castle he visited England, spent some time in London, and became a favorite at court, being much noticed by Queene Anne for his beauty — of which the

---

* The tradition is that it was built by Charles I.

Rev. John Emerson

reader may form some opinion from our copy of his portrait.* Through her admiration for Mr. Emerson, Queen Anne became a patron of his church at New Castle, and sent frequent gifts to it. He was dismissed from the church in 1712, and in 1715 installed over the South Parish of Portsmouth. Mr. Emerson was a native of Gloucester, Mass., and a graduate of Harvard College in 1689, at nineteen years old. How did he happen to come to New Castle? One of his classmates, Samuel Moody, was from here, and class associations have something to do with the distribution of members; then he owned some landed property in New Castle, bought of his father, who was the guardian of Nathaniel Martin of this town. By such slight circumstances, doubtless, he became connected with the place, and they led to his settlement as its minister. He preached in Portsmouth until his death, in 1732; the church there increased greatly in his time. Earthquakes have their uses, their bright side; that of 1727 added forty members at once to his church.

As soon as Mr. Emerson had been dismissed from the New Castle church, the town made an application to the President of Harvard College, John Leverett, for a suitable minister for the place. He recommended one John Tuck. But for some reason not now clear, the town did not take him. Rev. William Shurtleff was the successful candidate, and was installed in 1712; and it was voted "that Mr. Shurtleff should have £65 per year for his annual salary during ye time he lives single; but when his family increases by marriage he shall have £80 per year." Now, we had in New Castle at that period our incipient aristocracy, made up, as usual, of grocers, fish-dealers and inn-keepers, at the head of which stood the Atkinson family, who wrote their name with two t's, and many beautiful flourishes, and doubtless wanted it accented on the last syllable. Mary Atkinson was the daughter of the house, and, I conjecture, engaged to Mr. Shurtleff, and the secret of his call and settlement, and of the vote given above, in regard to increase of salary on increase of family. At any rate, the heiress and beauty of the town married, according to the custom still maintained at this end of New Hampshire, the young and rising minister.

---

*The painter of this portrait is unknown; but was probably one of the Court artists of Queen Anne.

Her wealth and beauty were thought none too much for the
saintly Mr. Shurtleff, although she carried her head pretty high
and her temper was not the sweetest. There is good ground for
believing the new minister soon regretted his days of single
blessedness and £65, especially when he found, just as the Sabbath bell was on the last strokes, and the last sentence written,
that his study door was fast, and no way out except by climbing;
or, when he tasted his broiled mackerel peppered with his own
snuff. It was enough to try a saint, and his reputation for
meekness and patience, already great, was much increased in
the parish. People smiled a little, but took sides, of course,
with the parson: and it gave a point to his sermons, especially
those on the Beatitudes. In the dim old chronicles, methinks I
faintly recognize that modern apology, incompatibility — the
saintly, studious clerk, yoked to the handsome and lively girl.
Your sinner is the better man for beautiful women. However,
Mary Atkinson grew soberer with years; and when her husband
was called to Portsmouth — it was the customary way in those
days, to fledge your ministerial wing at New Castle, and then get
a call to Portsmouth — nothing more is heard of her giddy manners. One can imagine the final suppression of her nature in the
formal and freezing air of that neighborhood. She bequeathed an
elegant silver tankard, to be transmitted to her husband's successors in the South Parish; and it is still passed to each new
incumbent. Perhaps she intended it as a token of reconciliation,
a loving-cup. Let us think so, and drink from it to the memory
of the proud and handsome heiress of New Castle. Those who
prefer sermons can find several of Mr. Shurtleff's extant. He
was a graduate of Harvard College in 1707, and died, 1747. He
remained minister at New Castle about twenty-one years, and
succeeded Mr. Emerson in Portsmouth, as he did in New Castle.
Near the middle period of his term in this town, 1720, his salary
was increased to £100. The vote reads: "That Mr. Shurtleff
have £20 per annum added to his salary, to make up the sum of
£100 per annum, & so *de anno in annum* during his life." Eight
citizens publicly protested against this increase of salary. Pos-
sibly, the "per annums" and "*de anno in annum*," puzzled their
simple minds. The vote has a generous sound; and, indeed, was
the largest sum ever voted any minister of New Castle, before
or since. During Mr. Shurtleff's ministry, the town, having

often discussed the building of a parsonage, at length bought a house for that purpose, for £80. It is no longer in existence; it stood nearly opposite the church, and the well belonging to it is still in use; it is known as the "parsonage well," and is a neighborhood property, where folks get a bucket of water and as much gossip as they can carry home.

The next minister of the town was the Rev. John Blunt, born in Andover, Mass., and a graduate of Harvard College, in the large and distinguished class of 1727. He was ordained here December 20th, 1732, and remained pastor of the church until his death, August 7th, 1748. He did not live long enough to receive the usual call to Portsmouth, but long enough to become much endeared to the people of New Castle. Perhaps there was never a more excellent pastor, or more useful citizen in the history of the town. During his ministry there was a revival of religion, in which forty members were added to the church. Like his predecessor, he married into a notable family, whose name has been honorably associated with New Castle from about 1700 to the present time, the Frosts. Madam Sarah Blunt, so she was always called after her marriage, was the daughter of Hon. John Frost, member of His Majesty's Council, and commander, for a period, of a British man-of-war. His wife was Mary Pepperell, sister to Sir William. The daughters of this family were celebrated for their amiability and intelligence. One died in the splendor of early womanhood. Some member of the family, I suspect Madam Sarah Blunt herself, wrote excellent poetry. Two specimens are extant; and though of the gravestone order, are so much beyond its usual quality, that I must not pass them by, especially as they were inscribed on monuments once on New Castle graves. The first is in memory of the young lady above mentioned, Abagail Frost.

> "Released from cares, at rest she lies,
> Where peaceful slumbers close her eyes.
> Her faith all trials did endure,
> Like a strong pillar, firm and sure.
> Did adverse winds tempestuous roll,
> Hope was the anchor of her soul.
> We, by the olive in her hand,
> Her peaceful end may understand;
> And by the coronet is shown,
> Virtue, at last, shall wear the crown."

The second is in honor of Rev. John Blunt, the subject of the foregoing sketch, the fourth clergyman of New Castle, who married the sister of Abagail Frost, and died August 7th, 1748, aged 42.

> "Soft is the sleep of saints; in peace they lie;
> They rest in silence, but they never die;
> From these dark graves, their flesh refined shall rise,
> And in immortal bloom ascend the skies.
> Then shall thine eyes, dear Blunt, thine hands, thy tongue,
> In nicer harmony each member strung—
> Resume their warm devotion, and adore
> Him, in whose service, they were joined before."

Upon his death, the town voted to continue his salary to Madam Blunt for nine months, and appropriated forty dollars toward his funeral expenses; enough to cover charges for coffin, rings, gloves, rum and pipes. Tobacco you were expected to bring yourself. The funeral baked meats were also paid for by the town. The items are curious —

> "A barrel of Cider, ... £3
> A dozen of Cabbages, ... 1 16s
> A bushel of Turnips, ... 1"

The people contributed to the dinner as well, sending all sorts of dainties, as to a picnic. Rev. John Blunt had six children, three daughters and three sons, most of whom married, and had between them about forty children, who kept on multiplying in the same ratio, until, had they all remained in New Castle, the little island could have contained nobody else. But they spread abroad, and adorned other parts of our country; for the family, whose origin was in New Castle, numbers among its representatives many distinguished men. John Blunt, however, the third son of the New Castle clergyman, remained here, and was a shipmaster and farmer. He had six sons and three daughters. He taught these six sons, and one other boy, Thomas E. Oliver, navigation, in his own house, and every one of them became masters of vessels. The father was a short, stout man, and very emphatic in all his ways. He was a stern believer in Calvinism and the Revolution, and made good his faith with his loud and trumpet voice. He was a delegate from New Castle to the first assembly called at Exeter, in the Revolution. When his last son was born he took him in due time to be christened, to the New Castle Church, then under the charge of Rev. Stephen Chase, a Tory in his sympathies. The Captain had decided on the name William for his new boy; but the preacher pointed his opinion of the revolutionary tendencies of the time, by a sermon against Cromwell, just as Le meant New Castle sinners when he reproached the Jews. The sermon ended, the child was handed up. "What is the name?" whispered the minister. "Oliver Cromwell." "What did you say?" "OLIVER CROMWELL," thundered the old Captain, bringing down his cane till the church rung.* The square pews were shocked; the sides and galleries tittered, and the town was all agog for weeks after. This incident happened in the same year that the Fort was captured by the Sons of Liberty; and one can imagine New Castle as not wanting in excitements during those months. One of my friends has taken Captain Blunt and his little Cromwellian, as the subject of a Fourth-of-July ode; and I trust the public will come to hear it in 1893, when New Castle proposes to celebrate the two hundredth anniversary of its incorporation.

The successor of Blunt, in the New Castle parish, was Rev. David Robinson, a native of Stratham, N. H., and graduate of Harvard College in 1738. He was ordained in less than three months after the death of Blunt; the date is November 30th, 1748, and he died November 18th, 1749, having been pastor of the church a little less than one year. I find no record concerning his ministry, save this: It was voted that he should have "one hundred and forty ounces of silver, at 20s per ounce, to be paid in bills of public credit—the use of the whole parsonage as dwelling house, gardens, barns, pastures, meadows, and whatsoever hath been given to the ministry, or set apart for the minister's use in this Parish; also the contributions of strangers on the Sabbath days." The salary was the usual one; although it represents £140, it must be divided by two to give the actual value of bills of credit of the period. The parsonage house was a large two-storied building, and the allowance of the whole of it to Robinson seems to imply that it was not always

---

* Brewster's Rambles, 1st series.

customary, and that probably the new minister had a large family. By this date, the lands attached to the office had grown to be quite a little farm. There was ground around the church and the parsonage house, and as much as twelve acres in the quarter called by the natives, *Outalong*. One other perquisite must be here noticed, the contributions of strangers. This was never large, but it was usually in cash; and something certainly and regularly to be counted on, for whatever strangers came into the Province, or passed through, quartered or rendezvoused in New Castle. This, I think, is clear, from the large number of inns always kept here. In addition, there were more or less vessels always at anchor in the harbor, whose officers and men came ashore on Sunday, and the tythingmen looked sharp that they did not spend the sermon time at the inns. The officers and soldiers at the Fort might be also counted among the cash contributors to the parson's Sunday collection; so that we must conclude his office more lucrative than any other in the Province for many years, and his nominal salary only a fraction of his real income.*

Of the next pastor, Rev. Stephen Chase, there is little to record, save dates and the anecdote already given, which shows that some New England clergymen were Tories. Mr. Chase was born in Newbury, Mass., and graduated at Harvard College, 1728. He was fifty years of age when installed over the New Castle church, in 1756, and remained its pastor for twenty-two years, or until his death. It appears that for seven years, that is, from the death of Robinson to the settlement of Chase, the church was without a minister; and that on the death of the latter there was another interregnum of six years. The probable explanation of these vacant periods, is the disturbed condition of the country, which was more immediately and severely felt here than elsewhere in New Hampshire.

In 1784, Rev. Oliver Noble undertook the pastoral office; and, I think, remained in it until his death, in 1792. In Mr. Noble we have for the first time connected with the church or town, a graduate of Yale College. He was of the class of 1757.

---

* I find that the church often had an appropriation from the Province, on account of the soldiers at the fort attending it. Altogether, it evidently was looked upon not as a local interest, but as the little St. Peter's of the country, to whose support the faithful of all parts were expected to contribute.

We have now reached the last name inscribed on the marble tablet placed, in 1852, in the front panel of the New Castle pulpit. There are six names in all; the absence of three other names belonging there, — Moody, Woodbridge and Jourdan, — all preceding Rev. John Emerson in 1703, can now be accounted for from the fact that when the tablet was erected the town records had not been recovered, and the earliest history of New Castle was unknown except by faint traditions.

After 1792, the church began to languish, and there was no settled ministry. In my narrative of the life of Benjamin Randall and his founding of the Free Will Baptist sect, I have spoken of the division that came in the old church, in consequence of that movement. That was one of the reasons of the decay of this ancient and venerable church. By 1821, it was reduced to a "visibility" of one member, whose name has been handed down to us, — Mrs. Mehitable White, widow of Capt. Robert White, and descended from the Sheafes.

Not only had the spiritual body of the church become almost extinct, but its earthly tabernacle was falling to ruins. In 1828, the ancient church, full of the memories of six ministers and four generations of worshippers, was taken down and a new one begun. It was not, however, finished, until 1835. In the spring of that year it was dedicated; Rev. Dr. A. P. Peabody delivered the address. The subsequent history of the society may be given in a brief summary: The pulpit of the new church was supplied by, first — Rev. Mr. Norris, Plummer, and others, until 1839; next, by a succession of clergymen recommended, and, in part, supported by, the New Hampshire Missionary Society, who preached here in the order of their names: James Hobart, Joseph P. Tyler, Jonathan Ward, Lucius Alden, Mr. Christie, Mr. Stone, B. F. Grant, and Mr. Williston.

Of these gentlemen, Rev. Lucius Alden remained longest, and became most identified with the town. He presided over the church and Sunday-school from 1846 to 1872. He was a direct descendant of John Alden, but never had the luck to be asked to speak for himself by any Priscilla, and remained steadfastly in his happy freedom, to devote all his mind and heart to this people. He was the most modest, gentle and reticent of men; yet, in the pulpit, where he felt the encouraging presence of his Master, and another message than of his own invention, his whole bearing and presence seemed to be changed; he spoke with boldness, with authority, and with fulness. For the rest, he went among his people, never as a guest or social friend, but only on errands of benevolence. It was not safe to speak disrespectfully of Parson Alden, even among men who never had heard him preach in the whole course of their lives. Such is the force of an upright, perfect character; it commands without effort, without contact, at a distance; the rumor of it even, goes to the hearts of men. Parson Alden was, without doubt, the last of the Puritans; he abated something of their strictness in behalf of others, but not for himself. He changed his wig on the Sabbath, but not his principles; all the week, under his every-day wig, he carried the same thoughts, the same conversation, the same purpose. In his old age, and toward the close of his labors here, he grew to resemble more and more the Puritan figure. He was tall, spare, very erect, and somewhat precise in his movements. He loved the island and its antiquities; and he was here just in season to obtain from several very aged people, facts and traditions reaching back almost to the earliest times, of which I have everywhere in this narrative availed myself. While he had charge of the church, he cultivated a flower-garden in the grounds attached to it, which gave pleasure to the passer-by, and caused him to wonder at the unusual sight. Mr. Alden was the model of the old-fashioned clergyman, wise in unworldly wisdom, and, though fulfilling a public office, leading always a retired and holy life. He was almost courtly in his manners, an old-school gentleman, and he commanded that consideration and respect which it was natural for him to bestow upon every human being. This was his most profitable example; and none is more needed in village communities, where a too great familiarity is a common habit, and leads to many evils. His example, his life and character, I dare say, came more nearly home to us than his sermons, which had the remoteness of another age, and an elevation which it was in vain for us to try to reach without those successive and more humble steps of morals, manners, and the ordering of our daily duties and conversation.

A pastor, however, who had married a whole generation of New Castle lovers, and attended the funerals of three hundred and forty of our inhabitants, might be excused if he looked on life from an ideal plane. But it is a matter of faith with me,

that a man who looks down from any sort of height teaches us
to look up. This notice would not be complete unless I should
add that Mr. Alden, though a wealthy man, lived after the most
frugal country style; a spare diet, a small attic room, few books,
plain clothing, without an indulgence —save one annual visit to a
Saratoga spring for his special distemper — gave him the means
of contributing liberally to the poor and those charities in which
he was interested. His name will be writ large in the Book of
Life. That, however, is not our affair; but it should be ours to
see to it that his name is inscribed upon the tablet of the New
Castle church, below — in the order of time, not merit — the
names of his six predecessors.*

As has been already stated, the first building for religious
purposes stood near the Fort, or Castle, as called in the old time.
Its date is unknown; its form and size I have been unable to
learn anything of. That it had at least one gallery — for
women, costing £3 — we know from an item in the town
accounts. There is little doubt it had a bell, which was removed
and hung in the belfry of the second church, and again to that
of the third. Several items in the town accounts for repairs on
the first church are given; among them is one which would be a
conundrum to those who had never seen or heard of our forefathers' means of hanging doors, with strap hinges of various
shapes, the more elaborate being in the form of the letter S; and
this is what is meant in the following item for 1695:

"*Town of New Castle,* Dr.
To 1 pair of *esses* to hang ye meeting-house door."

In regard to the second church, built about 1704, during Mr.
Emerson's settlement, I am able to give a more full description. There are several persons still living who remember it: in
particular, my friend, Capt. John Vennard, whom I introduced
to the reader in the village store, and whose excellent portrait
adorns this book. His extraordinary memory has usually supplied all my missing links; and I take this opportunity of
acknowledgment. This ancient citizen has pictured for me in

---

* Since writing the above Mr. Alden has died, at the age of eighty-eight years.
He graduated at Brown University, 1821.

capital detail, not only the building itself, but the spiritual body that was accustomed to worship therein. There was much in the interior decorations of the walls to excite the wonder and curiosity of a bright boy, who had never been out of his native village; and Capt. John would often steal in, when he could escape the tythingmen, and look for the hundredth time upon those great canvases, resplendent with red and blue angels. There was also, in large dimensions, the English coat of arms, which was undoubtedly a relic taken from the first church, and a slight evidence of the tradition of that church having been the gift of Charles I. Capt. John remembers the old couplet about the lion and the unicorn, inscribed under the coat of arms. There was also a splendid altar-piece, the gift of the first Lieutenant-Governor John Wentworth. Of all the many gifts which this church received from its noble and wealthy patrons at home and abroad, the bar placed above this altar-piece is all that remains.* It bears this inscription: "Ex Dono: the Hon. Jno. Wentworth: Lieut. Governor: June 1718." The building had galleries around three sides; the high and spacious mahogany pulpit was at the western end, and over it hung a sounding-board, ornamented with paintings of scriptural scenes. The central portion of the church contained square pews, for the gentry, with ornamental spindle-work rails; around the sides sat the humbler sort of folks. The "seating" of this church when it was new and first occupied, in the beginning of the eighteenth century, was a very delicate, troublesome undertaking. For your pew told your rank, or, your money. I find many votes passed in regard to this business, some of which are unmistakably the expression of somebody's personal pique; others what, in old-fashioned phrase, was called the "sense of the meeting." To get a square pew and find themselves seated in it, gave those "early Christians" the same sense of superiority and satisfaction that an opera box gives their descendants. The idea of distinction by separation, pervaded not only society and the church, but ran through all the points of their religious beliefs; heaven itself should be a sort of square pew, with, perhaps, a little higher spindle-rail and a softer cushion.

---

* The ancient cups and bread salver of the communion service, given by Mrs. Jane Turrell, a sister of Sir W. Pepperell, have been melted over into modern style. Alas!

Three tythingmen, elected at town-meetings regularly, from 1693 to 1839, attended the mighty men of New Castle to their pews; and kept order before and during service. With their long staves they touched the noses of drowsy people, and whacked the shoulders of sinners and boys. It was also their business to see that the Sabbath was kept. But during sermon-time, the constable of the town, and one householder of good standing, were ordered "to walk to every public house in town to suppress ill orders, and if they think convenient to private houses also." Sunday was a very still day. You could not visit your neighbor without danger of being called to an account, even as late as 1830. Capt. John relates the narrow escape that both he and his father had, when the latter sent him out, one Sunday, to borrow a piece of tobacco. Men were not permitted to loaf at the boat-landings; nor could they gather around the doors of the closed shops, as now, like cattle shut out of a barn. O for the good old times! The minister's black servant, usually a slave, had the office of sexton; and, for many years, I find a vote "to Cuffy 10s for the care of ye meeting-house." He rang the bell. A word as to this bell, — according to all accounts the sweetest ever heard in these parts. The natives believed it to be pretty much all silver. It was a gift of the English government, the loot of some of its continental wars. Its music reached every part of the island, and across the nearer waters. Cuffy was said to have a fine ear; and to be able to ring a clearer, sweeter tone than anybody else. His funeral stroke brought him an extra allowance of funeral rum, and the admiration of all the mourners. In fact, you were not well buried without his tolling you to the grave. Its inscription was in a foreign tongue, but what one, or what it was, I cannot discover, as the generation which remembers the old bell are not linguists.

At last it rang out its own death knell. Many a time had it called the citizens to arms, to prayers, to death, to town meetings, to the arrival of a new governor. On the 29th October, 1727, when everybody was shaking with terror at an earthquake, what should be heard but its voice from the belfry; and people thought it was a dreadful omen. It sounded the peace of the Revolution, from sunrise to sunset; and tolled the death of Washington, and his funeral. In 1812, it summoned the people to build Walbach Tower, and to defend their shores from

British ships, approaching from Appledore. Then it was weary, old and worn; but when the news of peace with England, in 1816, reached New Castle late one evening, by a post-rider, dispatched from Boston to Col. Walbach, at the Fort, it pealed once again and all night long, and in the morning became silent forever.

Not many years after, the old church itself, disconsolate at the loss of its life-long companion, the bell, and tired of the reproach of being old-fashioned and out of date, gave place to a new building. This happened in 1828. About that time there was a very enterprising carpenter in New Castle, who had an ardent desire to reconstruct the town generally, on the soap-box model; and he succeeded to a deplorable extent. It was, however, too early for a perfect success; and, let us thank heaven, it was before the days of the American renaissance. Our carpenter built a new church which is not remarkable; but it is not pretentious, and it has a simple and rather well-proportioned interior, as the reader will see from the picture. Here one may worship, undisturbed either by its ugliness or splendors; and if his mind wanders from his devotions at all, it can only be in reverent recollection of the innumerable congregations which have here succeeded each other, coming together in companies, but destined to depart singly and unattended.

> "From humble tenements around
>   Came up the pensive train,
> And in the church a blessing found
>   That filled their homes again.
>
> They live with God; their homes are dust;
>   Yet here their children pray,
> And in this fleeting life-time trust
>   To find the narrow way."

SECULAR AFFAIRS

ECULAR affairs are a much more safe and agreeable subject for the local historian than religious. I fear, in some of the preceding pages, I have fallen into a too gay and uncertain manner, which immediately one wishes to atone for, by a surrender to the spirit which is never very far from any one of us, but which has its hardest encounter with man when he takes up the pen of a town historian. But the fault is not wholly mine, if it has been difficult to maintain an even and sober step among the religious annals of the community; the fault is its own, for it is not able to lay aside altogether its weaknesses and absurdities, its human personality, even in the presence of the Impersonal.

It has been difficult also, in the preceding pages, to separate the history of New Castle from the general affairs of the Province of New Hampshire in the early times. We may naturally claim whatever transpired here, as the building of forts, the entry and clearance of vessels, the residence of governors and the meetings of councils and assemblies, as a part of the town's history. New Hampshire has forgotten that story; or, when she remembers, is apt to locate it at Portsmouth. The fact is, that the settlement of New Castle was prior to that of Portsmouth; and that for the first seventy-five years, it was the capital of the Province, and two-thirds of the provincial officials citizens of the town. This is conclusively shown in the first two volumes of the New Hampshire Provincial Papers. That anyone should be born to set this matter right, at this late day, may provoke a smile, and be credited to the usual indiscretion of magnifying the office of town chronicler. But I have no consuming ambition of that sort which wishes to fix the facts of history beyond peradventure; they are much better in a nebulous, fabulous state. The early history of New Hampshire is more curious and amusing than important; and, in regard to that of New Castle, I never propose anything more serious than to discover all that belongs to it, with the faint expectation of identifying the same old story which meets us wherever we follow the footsteps of man. Considerable imagination is requisite, in an islander, I admit, to enlarge the town boundary to include his neighbors (I mean mankind) but —

> "If with fancy unfurled
> You leave your abode,
> You may go round the world
> By the 'Inalong' road."

There are two aspects, two periods, that chiefly make the history of New Castle interesting: the first is the town as the centre of all the principal events of the earliest provincial period; the other is when, left only to its own local affairs, it gradually became insular, clannish and peculiar.

In regard to the causes of its early importance and subsequent obscurity, they were altogether natural. Rarely does a colony remain on the precise spot where it first arrives. It looks about, and soon moves on to more advantageous seats. This continues indefinitely; yet, sometimes leaving behind seed enough for large and permanent communities, in favorable situations; at other times leaving a waste, or a feeble remnant, doomed to remain in insignificance, or slow decay. As soon as the colonists found out what were likely to be the natural resources and business of this part of New England, they planted themselves on this island, directly at the mouth of the Piscataqua, where the facilities for maritime affairs, for fisheries and Indian trade were most convenient. But in those days it was necessary to protect your property and your person by defences of some sort at exposed points. Now an island affords the most natural and easiest opportunities of defence. Anyone who will look at the map of this island, on page vi, which has been drawn and reduced from the government survey map, will observe that its form is already that of a fort, very nearly square, with jutting points of land at the four angles, like bastions. Now, rude fortifications were early built on these four corners, which immediately gave the island still more the appearance of a great coast defence. The first was constructed by Capt. Walter Neale, between 1630 and 1640, whether in anticipation of a settlement here, or because of the natural advantages of defence; or, as is more probable from facts already stated, in order to protect the families already settled along the shore from the Indians, or a worse enemy, the white pirates who infested the coast. Nearly through the whole provincial period, it was the settled determination of the people and the officials, to construct a system of defences from Fort Point to Jaffrey Point, and thence to the narrowest part of Little Harbor, at the place where now the free bridge crosses it. For this purpose men were drafted, in seasons of the year when farm-work was not pressing, from all the towns in the Province to labor upon the defences. They were drawn in rotation from the towns, and worked from ten to twenty days each.* They were fed and sheltered, while so employed, by the families of New Castle, sometimes at the expense of the whole Province, at others, of the town. It was the duty of New Castle to keep a constant guard at the main Fort, or Castle, of from four to six men; and aslo a watchman on Jaffrey Point, and one or two in the vicinity of the free bridge. On this account the town was generally exempted from the levies for other military duty; and also often excused from payment of Province rates, or they were reduced to a merely nominal sum in its favor. New Castle was the pet of the Province; looked upon as a common possession, a barrier town, a place of refuge in case of extreme danger or disaster. So much for the military situation.

Its means of protecting itself and its consequent importance, were the reasons for its selection as the residence of governors and the meeting-place of the Provincial Assemblies, as soon as the Province had a government of its own.

In order to gratify the prejudice of my historical friends for

---

*The proportion for each of the five towns of the Province was, in 1704, as follows: Hampton, 13 men; Exeter, 11 do.; Portsmouth, 11 do.; Dover, 9 do.; New Castle, 4 do.

facts and evidence. I have, with infinite labor, collated all the extant documents, and performed a very long sum in addition, whose condensed result is this:

Whole number of Assemblies, from 1681 to 1698, ... 83
Of which there were held at New Castle, ... 76
"   "   Portsmouth, ... 7

It is necessary to state that the jurisdiction of Massachusetts over New Hampshire began about 1641, and continued until the middle of the year 1679; but no actual local government was put in operation in New Hampshire before about 1680–81, so that there is little doubt the very first representative body ever convened in the State was at New Castle. For the first ten years of the new order of things, there were very infrequent meetings of the Provincial Assembly. Affairs were managed by a Council, which sat here most of the time for that period. In fact, the date of the first Council meeting is, Great Island, January 15th, 1683, and every one of its meetings was here until September 29th, 1692. All the members of this first recorded Council, including the governor, Edward Cranfield, lived at New Castle; their names were Robert Mason, Walter Barefoot, Richard Chamberlain (Secretary) Nathaniel Frier, Robert Elliot, and John Hinks.

During the years from 1692 to 1697, the Assembly met constantly at New Castle. I also find that the law courts sat here, the first on record bearing this heading: "At the Court of Pleas, held at Great Island, September 25th, 1683;" then follows a judgment in a suit between Walter Barefoot and Robert Wadley. This date is immediately following the promulgation of the earliest code. In the old records of this region, it is sometimes impossible to tell whether occurrences mentioned were in Portsmouth or New Castle. When said to be at Piscataqua, it may mean any one of several places; when the designation is Strawberry Bank, it means what was subsequently Portsmouth; but, after 1653, and until after 1693, when Portsmouth is named, it may be New Castle is meant as well. Thus the deputies from these parts to the General Court of Massachusetts, from 1653 to 1679, are recorded as from Portsmouth; but out of the twenty-four deputies so recorded between the above-mentioned years, eighteen were resident at New Castle.

After 1693, the date of the incorporation of New Castle, there is no confusion in the documents as to the names of places. The town henceforward sailed under its own colors; though still keeping, even to the present time, its larger, descriptive designation of Great Island.

In the preceding outline, it will be seen how much of our rightful history has been concentrated into a few sentences. The remainder must be left to the imagination of the reader, who will not fail to picture to himself all the characteristic features and doings of a small fortified island and first capital of a pigmy province, the resort of broken soldiers of fortune, of briefless London lawyers, of damaged ministers, land speculators and adventurers. A large and interesting volume might be compiled on this period alone, of New Castle history; and I am sure the reader will appreciate my reserve and the modest proportions of this book, when I tell him that town histories usually contrive to make not less than five or six hundred pages, out of much less material than has been at my disposal.*

The meetings of the Council were commonly held at the houses of some of its members, or at an ordinary, where meat and drink were convenient, in case of a prolonged session. The Assembly also met, at first, in private houses. In 1682–83, it met in the Jaffrey house. Subsequently the Atkinson house became the usual place of its meetings, and was known as the Province House. Its site, and a remaining portion, have already been alluded to and depicted. The Assemblymen were quartered in the inns of the town. By law, these were limited in any one place, to four; but here, the need being greater, a larger number were allowed. Inn-keeping was the most popular and lucrative sort of business in New Castle during most of the provincial period. As in other countries, the business descended in families, and when men failed, widows and daughters continued to

---

* It is true, their method is called by fleering critics (to whom *vita sine literis mors est*) padding. Cuts of first-class houses, and their successful owners, are the usual means of inflating the covers of town and county histories. I, too, should have been glad to have presented my readers with some portraits of the great men of New Castle, after the customary manner. But, alas, my fellow citizens are not abreast the times, and do not appreciate at what a moderate outlay of cash they could be immortalized. One representative parson, one representative skipper, and an ancient merchant, are all we could afford to give gratuitously. But the way is open — do you understand ? — in our next edition.

carry it on. Hannah Purmitt, or, Purmont, seems to have been the favorite landlady of the Councillors and Assemblymen, in the latter part of the seventeenth century. At her hostlery were good meat and drink; and her pretty maids assisted the mighty sovereigns of New Hampshire greatly, in putting off the cares of state. Inn-keeping was about the only business done on a cash basis. Corn and pork could not conveniently pay the score of glasses of rum and a night's lodging. Some of our most ancient, respectable citizens, were taverners, beginning with Samuel Wentworth, "at the sign of ye Dolphin," ancestor of three governors and an innumerable posterity. In fact, it was very difficult to procure a license unless the applicant was of good character and standing. The petitions for a license were always well larded with expressions of piety, to give a savor of decorous intention on the part of the petitioner. Here is a specimen of a petition for an inn at New Castle, of the date 5th September, 1682, from the original manuscript:

"Ye humble Petition*, Humphrey Spenser and Grace his wife humbly sueth that yr Honors would please to grant them Liberty for to entertain people for lodging, victualling & bear; we are accommodated by the blessing of God to do so much, and his providence hath so ordered it that strangers; — as often times there are many in the place & those as they say and we are subject to believe know not where to bestow themselves; comes to our house and having wherewithal to help them cannot denie it. But if we should do it all upon free gift may be at last in as great a streight as they if not worse. Therefore humbly craveth again that your honors give us our humble request who shall always Remain ready to pray for your honors prosperity & good success of this good government.

yo'r humble Petitioners,
HUMPHREY SPENSER,
GRACE " " "*

The ingenious argument of this petition — undoubtedly the hand of Mistress Grace — is delightful.

---

* Humphrey and Grace afterward fell into trouble and disgrace, in spite of the beautiful language of their petition.

The Councillors, mostly resident here, had their sessions whenever public necessity demanded; they were the executive department of the little government, and divided among themselves nearly all the offices; they were the justices of the peace, captains of the fort, treasurers, etc.; and when the Assembly met they also met, and were called the "Upper House." They were careful about calling the Assembly together, unless upon an extraordinary emergency. This made the New Castle innkeepers murmur; they said the people had no rights. But never was there a more unmanageable body, when they were assembled. The Governors could get nothing out of them in the way of financial legislation, though backed by the Council. They would either maintain a rigid silence, or send some equivocal answer. Once all their reply to a demand concerning the Fort, made by Governor Usher, was to send up this vote: "*See 14 Luke 28.*" They actually starved out all the Provincial Governors before the Wentworths. Nor could they be kept together if their own private concerns called them home. They found reason enough for adjournment when it was time to plant corn, or to harvest it. What charming simplicity!

But New Castle liked to have them in town; it made business lively. Every Assemblyman took occasion to lay in, while here, his family supply of dried fish, salt and rum, and he sampled the latter often, in order to be sure about his intended purchase. Besides, the town got all the favors it asked for; abatement of rates, appropriations for the church, relief from garrisoning the fort, and assistance in strengthening the island defences and maintaining ferries.

New Castle became a port of entry about 1686; and for one hundred years thereafter the shipping business was extensive. Consequently, the arrival and departure of vessels brought officers and men ashore, and gave plenty of business to taverners and animation to the town.

I must add, in conclusion, a custom I find common from the earliest times up to the Revolution, and occasionally afterward, that afforded the old town a frequent holiday. Whenever the English government declared war, or made a treaty of peace, or a royal personage died or was born, or a new king ascended the throne, the principal people of the Province assembled at New Castle to have a salute at the Fort, hear the proclamation read, and drink formal healths to all the parties, and end the day in drinking to each other's.*

As a port of entry and clearance, New Castle had a position at once honorable and dangerous. The customs regulations were crude, and the power of enforcing them unreliable. Every vessel escaped them if she could, and resisted when she dared. Vessels that belonged here thought themselves entitled to immunity, especially if owned by church members; and all the mast ships claimed a royal prerogative. If the Province collected any fees it was lucky; and how small the amount must have been is shown by the order of the General Court of Massachusetts, in 1672, that it should be appropriated for the support of the fort at New Castle; and the same order was made more than once after the Province had a government of its own. In the olden time, merchant vessels carried guns, and often as many as the fort mounted. But the little fort sent a shot across the bows of any vessel which had not paid its dues; and if the vessel submitted she was obliged not only to pay them, but also the cost of said shot. Vessels of forty tons register and upwards paid an entrance fee of about £5, and the same for clearance. Coasters paid, for a yearly bond, £5. Coasters were mostly sloop-rigged, and carried, when bound for Salem or Boston, two men; when for Virginia, four. Ketches were two-masted, larger than sloops, and better sailers. Then there were shallops, pinckes, and fly-boats.† There was, toward the close of the seventeenth century, a fly-boat called the America, trading constantly between this port and London. She was of three hundred tons burthen, mounted four guns and carried twenty men. Her commander

---

* I have found, in the New Hampshire archives, many MSS. throwing light on the customs of the time, the foregoing among others. The published Provincial Papers are mainly official; but one is astonished to find that even as such, they are only *selections*, badly arranged, and with an index not to be trusted, and orthography often differing from the original; while only a few of the Court records have been printed, and none of the documents and private papers which would give us a picture of the actual life of this Province in the seventeenth and eighteenth centuries, and afford an explanation of many obscurities in New Hampshire history.

† Fly-boats had a high stem and broad beam; pinckes, both high stem and stern, both sharp and looking alike. A few pinckes are still afloat — relics of a past age.

was John Holmes. She carried out to London mostly masts, oars, staves, furs, and once two barrels of "cranberrys," which I imagine was an experiment, perhaps the first and last from these parts. She brought back wrought pewter and brass and iron, groceries, dry goods, saddles, hats, farming tools, guns and shot. The coasters took a mixed freight, carrying from here lumber and fish, apples, cider, perry and cheese; and returning with all sorts of household goods and provisions. Their bills of lading were curious compounds of counting-room forms and pious references to divine providence. The reader may see, at the beginning of this chapter, an uncommonly fine specimen of an initial letter, copied from an ancient bill of lading. The whole word is "Shipped" — "Shipped by the Grace of God."

We have little accurate knowledge of the amount of shipping business in the earliest times; but it always must have been considerable, and steadily increasing. For ten months of the years 1680-81, forty-seven vessels were entered and cleared; which had increased, in one hundred years from the above date, to two hundred and sixty-seven. Although Boston and Salem were always reproaching this settlement for its mercenary spirit, they, none the less, were jealous rivals of the Piscataqua trade, and did what they could to injure it. A new era was expected when the Province was released from the control of Massachusetts and set up a governor, council and assembly of its own. The people could now wear long hair and do business without church membership, which had been interdicted since 1648. But the new government did not work at all smoothly. In fact, the people had become impregnated with Puritan notions; and began to snuff the spirit of freedom and political independence which were rife under the religious garb. The English government, foiled at every step in Massachusetts, thought to begin here a new system, and plant a power which should be an antidote to the neighboring malady. Cranfield's administration, though brief, is the most interesting of the Provincial period. His great effort was in the attempt to re-establish the English church. We must give him the credit of seeing the root of all the troubles between the colonists and England. He found it in the clergy, and especially in Harvard College, where they were bred.

He could obtain no convictions, for breach of the revenue laws, against church members. He therefore set about the attempt to remove the preachers; but the imprisonment of Moody (to which previous reference has been made) only deepened his difficulties. On visiting Boston, expressly to ferret out the secret springs of the factious spirit of his own colony, he made a wonderful discovery, which does a great deal of credit to his penetration. He found the seat of all evils at Cambridge; and thenceforth labored with the English government to take swift measures for the suppression of Harvard College. I give some extracts from his letters, recently discovered, and, perhaps, new to most of my readers :

"It will be necessary to dissolve their University of Cambridge, for from thence all the several colonies in New England are supplied; the people looking upon their teachers little less than apostles, it is incredible what an influence they have over the vulgar."

In another letter to his government he says :

"That there can be no greater evil attend his Majesty's affairs here, than those pernicious and rebellious principles which flow from their college at Cambridge, which they call their University; from whence all the towns, both in this and other colonies, are supplied with factious and seditious preachers, who stir up the people . . . so that I am humbly of opinion this country can never be well settled till their preachers be reformed and that college suppressed."

Cranfield was supported in his policy by Walter Barefoot and Richard Chamberlain. The former was a chief figure in New Castle history from 1660 to the close of the century. He held every office, at one time and another; yet was never popular, and has come down to us with a bad name. He was a brave soldier, and independent in thought and action. The witchcraft delusion did not delude him; and he rescued Quakers from persecution and death. The popular party undertook to suppress him, but failed signally. His only answer in court, on one occasion of arrest, to all and every question was, "*My name is Walter.*"

He commanded the fort for a long period; was a judge and justice of the peace, and a deputy governor. He boasted of his relation to all the wealthy families of the Province by marriage; but I can find no trace of it, nor of any of his descendants. Below are his signature and seal.

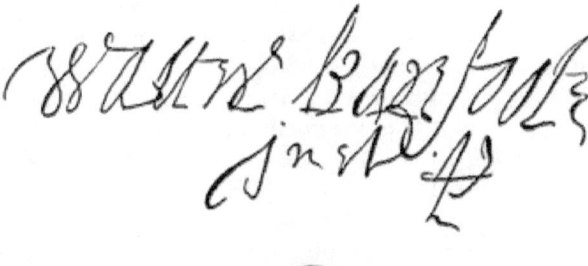

Richard Chamberlain was Secretary of the Province, and a resident of New Castle for some years. We are indebted to his pen for the account of the "stone-throwing devil," and also for nearly all the documents of interest concerning the Mason land contest and other affairs of the Province, while he was its secretary. He was fond of literature and the fine arts, and was an amateur musician. I judge from his handwriting that he loved form and order. There is before me a New Castle deed, written by him in 1685, on parchment, as fresh, clear and neat as if but of yesterday. The deed runs from Rich. Welcome and his wife Eleanor of Star Island, to Henry Beck of Great Island, and conveys a house forty feet square, and a small parcel of land, near the house of John Hunkin, situate on a highway running to the water-side.

Cranfield lived in New Castle, sometimes at an ordinary, at other times in private houses. He occupied the Jaffrey cottage for two years.

It was during the administration of Cranfield that the inhabitants of Great Island began to agitate the subject of incorporation. They had previously (date uncertain) obtained permission from the Massachusetts General Court to have a minister of their own. They now renewed the application to their own newly-constituted government. The request was simply "to have an allowed and approved minister among us;" whether at their own sole charge or that of the whole town, they left open for consideration. The people chose Nathaniel Fryer, George Jaffrey, Robert Elliot and John Hinks to present and enlarge upon their petition. The argument was the profanation of the Sabbath, abundance of children who could hear no sermons, servants who wanted ease on Sunday instead of the labor of rowing their masters and mistresses to the Portsmouth church, and, finally, the danger of leaving, for a single day, his Majesty's fortifications unprotected.

At this date, 1682, there were about sixty families on the island; ten wharves and twenty-six barns and warehouses. But the figures in regard to the population of this period are unreliable; for at about the same date, I find nearly one hundred names of men supposed to be living in New Castle. All the confusion prior to the Revolution, or, to be exact, 1773, arises from three circumstances: first, the fact of the place having an unusually large transient population, yet which reckoned themselves, on account of the unsettled state of this part of the country, as belonging where they happened to be; second, soldiers at the Fort, and men employed in construction of earthworks, at different times, were often counted in; and, lastly, the names of scattered families in that part of the township now Rye, and sailors and fishermen, sometimes at home and sometimes not, would be added to, or omitted from, petitions and enumerations of the population, according to chance.

For the gratification of genealogists and antiquarians, I will here append a list of such names as belong to the earliest history of New Castle. The selection is made from those appearing oftenest and remaining extant longest — some of them to the present time. The spelling of many of them is modernized. This is necessary, as the same name has often several forms, even when written by its bearer; and then, some of our ancestors had a singular autograph, made with two short lines crossing each other at various angles, while the spelling was done by some clerk or friend. But here is the list, arranged alphabetically; and I note that the name which stands first, has had that position, in increasing numbers, from 1680 to 1884:

Amazeen,	Parker,
Atkinson,	Rand,
Bell,	Randall,
Elliot,	Seavy,
Estwick,	Sheafe,
Fryer,	Stileman,
Hinckes,	Tarlton,
Jackson,	Trefethen,
Jaffrey,	Tucker,
Jones,	Waldron,
Jordan,	Walford,
Langmaid,	Wallis,
Leach,	Walton,
Odiorne,	White.

Let no one, who misses his name from the above list, feel aggrieved; but remember it is a selection of the more prominent of a certain early and limited period. The epoch of the Lears, Frosts, Sargents, Vennards, Prescotts, Meloons and Yeatons had not yet arrived.

Some of the names are fine; several uncommon. Our old friends Brown and Smith are conspicuously absent all through the town's annals; but we rejoice in a Jones, who, it is true, as yet, put that curious mark between his Christian and surname, but in time was able to write it in full against good round sums.

I have been struck in looking over New Castle genealogies, with the persistence of certain Christian names. As sure as there is a single Amazeen, his Christian name is John; if two, there is a John, Jr., or 2d. An Atkinson is always Theodore, and a Jaffrey, George, and a Sheafe, Sampson; while it would almost seem as if there could not be a Lear, whose first name was not Tobias. Whenever there is an Estwick, it is Pheasant. Jonathan clings to Odiorne, and Elias to Tarlton, through all generations. There is always a William Wallis. Later, Stileman got to be a Christian name, and continues to be; and is also perpetuated in the first ledge marked with a nun buoy, one-third of the way between the Fort and Whale's Back Light, known as Stileman's Rocks.

But the most remarkable concurrence of first names is in the Bell family, which, when blessed with sons, always called them, in due order of birth, Shadrach, Meshach and Abednego. All three bloom out together frequently in the town records, and once begin again with Shadrach, Jr. What whim possessed the founder of the family to burden his posterity with the uncouth appellations of those three ancient salamanders, I know not, unless the family tree was as old as Nebuchadnezzar's grass.

In consequence of this recurrence of the same Christian names for two hundred years in our history, it is often difficult to distinguish between members of the same family; and one is never certain which of certain individuals is intended in the documents.

In the foregoing list, I have omitted, purposely, the names of those families living within the boundaries of New Castle, but remote, and scattered all over the present territory of Rye. They were not closely identified with the island population, beyond attendance at the New Castle church, and ultimately formed a township, or parish of their own. Their names appear as remonstrants, whenever the strictly island people petitioned for a town charter. The leading families, who called themselves "Inhabitants at Sagamore creek," were the Berys, Bracketts, Langdons, Sherburnes, Lears, Slopers and Peverlys.

From 1682 to 1693, several petitions were offered by the people of the island for a township charter; but, being opposed by Portsmouth, as well as by the dwellers on Sagamore Creek, it was not granted. For some years before 1693, the people had refused to pay any tax assessed by Portsmouth; and at length the Governor and Council decided that such assessment was illegal. Having gained this important concession, the obtaining a charter was no longer difficult, and followed almost immediately. The first vote was taken 17th March, 1693, and was a tie on the part of the Council, but Lieutenant-Governor Usher decided it by voting yea. When the matter came up again, the grant meanwhile having been prepared and engrossed, there was but one dissenting vote upon its being signed and executed by the Lieutenant-Governor. So, on the 30th day of May, 1693, Great Island became "a Towne Corporate, by the name of New Castle, to the men and inhabitants thereof forever," on the payment to the King, or his successors, yearly, on the 20th October, of one peppercorn.

But the reader may like to see the whole of this, probably the oldest New England royal charter which has been preserved. The parchment is uninjured, and the writing is still decipherable.* The seal has been gone from it beyond the memory of the living. A copy, however, of the royal seal in use in this Province at the date of signing of this charter, and undoubtedly the same as originally affixed to the document, is given below.†

---

* By consent of the town, the original charter will be on exhibition at Hotel Wentworth, during the season of 1854.

† Medallists may like to know that this seal was the first in the history of this Province. In 1710, by order of her Majesty, Queen Anne, it was broken up, and a new one substituted, differing but slightly from the former, which continued in use until the Revolution.

CHARTER OF THE TOWN OF NEW CASTLE.

William and Mary, by the Grace of God, of England, Scotland, France and Ireland, King and Queen, Defenders of the Faith, &c., to all people to whom these presents shall Come Greeting. Know yee that Wee of our especiall Grace, certain knowledge, and meer motion, have Given and Granted And by these presents as farr as in us lyes, Doe give and Grant to our beloved Subjects, Men and Inhabitants, within and upon Great Island, within our Province of New Hampshire, in New England, and the lands to them belonging, Running from a point of Land there on the South side of Saggamores Creek, called Sampsons point, and from thence Southwest by the outside of the fenced land of Saggamores Creek to the head of Aaron Moses field to an old Hemlock Tree by the side of the Road way, and from thence upon the aforesaid Southwest point to the Road way, between Sandy Beach and Greenland, leaving Greenland about three miles to the Westwards soe forwards upon the same point to Hampton Bounds, and then East to the Sea, that the same be a Towne Corporate by the name of New Castle to the men and Inhabitants thereof forever. And Wee doe by these presents Give and Grant unto the said Men and Inhabitants of our towne of New Castle, all and every, the streetes, lanes and highways within the said Towne, for the Publique use and service of the Men and Inhabitants thereof and travellers there, together with full power, lycence and authority to the said men and inhabitants within the said towne forever, to establish, appoint, order and direct the establishing, making, laying out, ordering, amending and repairing of all streetes, lanes, highways, ferry places and Bridges, in and throughout the said Towne, necessary, needful and convenient for the Men and Inhabitants of the said towne, and for all travellers and passengers there: Provided always that our said Lycence soe as above granted for the establishing, making and laying out of streetes, lanes, highways, ferry places and Bridges, be not extended or constructed to extend to the taking away of any person or persons Right or Property without his, her, or their consent, or by some knowne law of our Province: To have and to hold and enjoy, all and singular, the premisses aforesaid, to the said Men and Inhabitants of the said Towne of New Castle and their successors forever, Rendring and paying therefore unto us, our heirs and successors, or to such other office or officers as shall be appointed to receive the same yearly, the annual quitt rent or acknowledgement of Owne Peppercorn in the said Towne, on the five & twentieth day of October, yearly, forever. And for the better order, rule and government of the said Towne Wee doe by these presents Grant for us and our successors unto the men and Inhabitants of the said Towne, That yearly and every year upon the first Tuesday of March, forever, they, the said men and Inhabitants of our said Towne shall elect and choose by the major part of them two sufficient and able men, householders in the said Towne, to be Constables for the year ensuing, which said men so chosen and elected shall be presented by the then next precedeing Constables to the next Quarter Sessions of the Peace, to be held for the said Province, there to take the accustomed oaths appointed by Law for the Execution of their offices, under such penaltyes as the Law of our said Province shall appoint and direct upon refusall or neglect therein. And Wee doe by these presents Grant for us, our Heirs and successors, unto the men and Inhabitants of the said Towne, That yearly and every year upon the said first Tuesday of March, forever, they, the said men and Inhabitants of our said Towne, or the major part of them, shall elect and choose three men, Inhabitants and householders, within our said Towne, to be overseers of the poor and highways, or selectmen for our said Towne, for the year ensueing, with such powers, priviledges and authorities as any overseers or selectmen within our said Province have and enjoy or ought to have and enjoy. And Wee doe further by these presents Give and Grant for us, our Heires and successors, unto the men and Inhabitants of the said Towne and their successors, forever, That they shall have and enjoy and use the Ferry the days of the Fairs of New Castle, aforesaid, forever, to be held there every Wednesday, and one Fair for two dayes, to witt, on the first Tuesday and Wednesdayes of July, forever, together with all issues and profits to the said Market and Fair accrewing or happening, and all liberties and free customs, priviledges and emoluments to the said Market and Fair belonging or appertaining: To have and to hold the said Market and Fair with issues and profits and liberties and free customs, priviledges and emoluments to the same or either of them accrewing or happening, belonging or appertaining to the said men and Inhabitants of our said Towne of New Castle and their successors, forever. In testimony whereof Wee have caused the Seal of our said Province to be hereunto affixed. Witness, John Usher, Esqr., our Lievetennt. Governor and Commander in Chiefe of our said Province at our said Towne of New Castle, the thirtyeth day of May, in the fifth year of our Reigne, Annoque Domi, 1693.

JN. USHER.

By the Lievt. Governours Command,
THEO. DAVIS, *Sec'ry*.

What was the population of New Castle at the date of this charter, it is quite impossible to determine accurately. On one occasion, forty men sign the petition; on another, thirty-three; and there are seventeen remonstrants. None of the government officials, who were citizens, appear to have thought it proper to sign a document on which they would have to act judicially. I think it would be safe to say that not more than one-third of the ratable citizens (men over sixteen years of age) signed any one of the petitions. It is probable, therefore, that in 1693 there were within the whole territory of the town not far from five hundred inhabitants. The right of fairs and market days, appointed in the charter, was probably never exercised; it was a conventional concession, according to old English custom. This charter continues to be the only authoritative legal sanction of the corporation of New Castle; and under its provisions our town-meetings are still held.

In the first part of the present century, an attempt was made to change the date of the annual town-meeting; but the people rebelled against it and kept their old custom.

In regard to the name of the town, I shall say little, because without positive proof of its origin. It would be most natural to suppose it borrowed from an English place name, or from the baronial title. But this Province had no associations with the English New Castle; and it was not until long after that any Duke of New Castle became connected with American colonial affairs. It is true, the title of New Castle had not lapsed; but it had, in 1693, no representative, for Thomas Hollis Pelham was born in 1694. Having eliminated those two possible sources of the origin of the name, what have we left? Only this: that, in common allusions to the Fort, it was often called "The Castle," and had its first distinctive name of Fort William and Mary not until one year after the incorporation of the town, that is, in 1694. It was then so named, probably, because about 1692 the king made the colony a present of some great guns, which were mounted on the old Fort. In addition to this new ordnance, the Fort was at about the same date repaired; and there seems to have been a foreign engineer employed in directing the mounting of the guns and general reconstruction of the works. My argument then, is simply this: the Fort had been called and known for a long period as "The Castle;" at the date of incorporation, it was furnished with new guns and substantially rebuilt, becoming a *new castle*. What more natural presumption, under these circumstances, than that the citizens and officials should give to the words constantly on their lips, the dignity of capital letters, NEW CASTLE, and thus establish a name, significant of the town's military importance — " the key," or " Castle," as they always called it, " of the Province ? " *

Twelve years ago, it would have been impossible to have continued this humble history after the date of incorporation, and for the next thirty-three years; or, from 1693 to 1726. The town records for that period were gone, none knew where; and many people were sceptical in regard to there ever having been any. But in the autumn of 1873, the postmaster of New Castle, H. M. Curtis, Esq., received a letter from Mr. Henry Starr, of London, informing him that one of his neighbors, a Captain Bokenham, of Cheshunt, in Hertfordshire, had in his possession two volumes of the town records of New Castle. The information was received here with considerable astonishment, and some incredulity. Some thought the British lion wanted to put his paw into our small dish; others, that it was a device for a large appropriation at the next town-meeting. However, the letter was cautiously answered, inquiry being made as to the expense of getting back the precious documents. The reply was the volumes themselves, by the next English mail. They proved to be our long-lost records, of the first thirty-three years of the town's corporate existence, in perfect preservation, and in the

---

* The reader will note that the above explanation is wholly theoretical. I am indebted to Isaac W. Hammond, Esq., Assistant Secretary of State for New Hampshire, a gentleman very learned and competent in all such curious inquiries, for a different theory in regard to the naming of New Castle. I present his view with pleasure; but it cannot be expected that I shall give the whole of the argument by which he overthrows my opinion; I will, however, print the positive part of what he writes me.

" As a rule, towns, etc., in those times, were named for places in Great Britain, or for some of the English nobility, with the exception of those which retained their Indian names; there were some exceptions, but I think no more than enough to prove the rule. There is a similarity in the situation of the city of New Castle, in the north of England, with reference to the river and ocean, and our town of New Castle. From this ancient English city came the title bestowed upon William Cavendish (Duke of New Castle) and in memory of him, in consequence of the similarity above mentioned, or both, came the name of our 'New-Castle-by-the-Sea," in my humble opinion."

handwriting of Francis Tucker, an attorney of New Castle; Theodore Atkinson, the first of that name; and Sampson Sheafe, probably the second of that name. The first volume is bound in vellum; the second has lost its binding, — perhaps never had any. No one knows, at present, when or how they got to England. Their discoverer, Mr. Henry Starr, supposes they were part of booty carried from New Castle in the Revolution; others have concluded they were taken to England to establish titles, or verify family descent. One theory is as good as another. The most curious part of the story is that Captain Bokenham, in whose house the records were found, did not at all know how they came there.

The discovery and return of these records was an almost romantic event for our little town, which had, indeed, some vague idea that its ancient history was more remarkable than its modern, but could not hitherto produce any evidence of it. The records were all the more indispensable to its earliest history, inasmuch as those of Portsmouth, which might have shed some light upon it, were known to have been destroyed. The town, at its next annual meeting (March, 1874) passed a handsome vote of thanks to the gentlemen who had discovered and presented the volumes, which was engrossed on parchment and forwarded to them in due time.

We have now a complete roll of town records, from 1693 to the present time, with the exception of the Revolutionary period, when the town was in confusion, and its public affairs were either neglected or no record was kept of them. The recovered documents have cleared up some obscurities, and corrected several mistakes in former references to the history of New Castle, the advantage of which has enabled me, in the preceding narrative, to follow the general course of events with more sequence and certainty; and now I shall summarize, briefly, the remaining portion of the town's history, confining myself to its local affairs chiefly, as they from this time forward became less mingled with those of the whole Province.

The charter having been issued on the 30th May, 1693, the regular procedure seems to have required that the Council should give leave to the citizens of the new enclosure to elect all necessary officers " for carrying on the prudential affairs of the town," which accordingly was granted, August 4th, in the same year.

But matters moved with great deliberation in those old days; and it was not until the 20th December, 1693, that the first town-meeting was held. The only officers elected at this time were three selectmen, John Clark, James Randel and Francis Tucker; and one constable, John Leach. The first business transacted was the levying a tax of £25 9s, of which £23 6s 8d was for the Province, "for repair of fortifications and reimbursing ye treasurer," and £1 14s 1d for the town's exclusive use. This was the sum of the first town tax; that of the current year, 1884, two hundred and one years later, is $3.000. But it was with the fathers as with us; they exceeded their appropriation; they actually spent £2 3s; and there was an alarming deficit of eight shillings and one pence! They had forgotten, in fact, to forecast the expense of a pair of stocks, which the credit and security of a new town required, and which cost £1 5s. Then there was that inevitable "contingent expense," and I seem to hear our old, first board of selectmen, as I have so often their successors, saying amidst much excitement, "it is not our fault that the windows of ye meeting-house had to be mended; the bill was 10s; we've paid Simpson's bill and got his receipt; now if you don't like it, stick your old hats into the next hole in ye old meeting-house." This meeting was held in the ancient church, near the Fort; it was December; and I fancy the new-made citizens, in knee-breeches and camlet cloaks, looking up at the windows, and, on the whole, glad to pay for the glazing. Still, they there and then began that wonderful enterprise of self-government, which has turned out so famously and grown to such extraordinary proportions, by thus early holding their rulers responsible for every public action and expenditure; yes, by themselves feeling accountable, and therefore having a personal interest in all public concerns.

I have spent the larger part of my life in the country, and began to go to town-meetings when the good red buns, and town-meeting cake and outside assemblage of boys, were the chief attractions. This old habit I have continued, partly from duty, believing, as one must, that these humble, local assemblies will be the last, as they were the first, refuge of the lovers of freedom among our race; and partly, I dare say, because I am still fond of buns and boys, and seeing how sensible or ridiculous men can be when assembled to deliberate and act on public affairs. Those of my readers, therefore, who have never attended a New England town-meeting, may be pleased to know what it is like.

In general, it may be said, that it is an occasion when some public business is transacted, of the necessary sort, and the year's accumulation of criticism, grievances and personal grudges be discharged. In New Castle we deliberate with our hats on, after the manner of the British Parliament. We always think here that it is time enough to take them off when we go to bed. No sooner is a new town government elected than it begins to be watched and found fault with. Then appears that almost natural impulse of our race, or, perhaps, inherited in its long contests for freedom, which impels it to consider its civil rulers natural enemies. In town governments this watchfulness and criticism are not always an unmixed good; they often become frivolous, and turn on personal or party sympathies and antipathies. As in a larger sphere, whoever holds a town office is almost sure to make more enemies than friends; and he is much more liable to know and feel it than office-holders of higher rank. One can better bear the mendacities and innuendoes of the press than the frowns and gossip of his neighbors and the village shop. If you wish to lose credit and good-will among your fellow-citizens, to discover your weaknesses, and to know the worst that can be said of you, go, get yourself into town office. "How can I find my family history?" said a gentleman to a genealogist. "Simply by running for office," was the answer. There is, in consequence, often a disinclination for town offices, as the emoluments are small and the risks great. The best men take them with some dread, not of the labors and duties, but the odium. It is not, however, deep-seated, abiding odium; it is quickly forgotten. It seems to be, in country communities, a sort of sportive revenge they delight in taking upon one of their own number, with whom they feel a perfect equality, for having set him in a little brief authority over themselves; as some savages whip their home-made gods.

I know of no more grim, and yet humorous spectacle among our various political assemblages, than the annual New England town-meeting. The selectmen are seated behind a long table, on which are the records, the account-books and papers, and a law-book or two — the Town Officer, perhaps, and the Statutes of the State. They look nervous, but defiant. Indeed, it does put a man on his mettle to face a body of citizens to whom he is directly accountable. Before the selectmen stand their fellow-citizens — perhaps fifty, perhaps two hundred, — ready to listen to the report of the year's transactions; ready, also, to put the most provoking questions. Many of them have been town officers themselves; these know the situation, but have the less mercy on that account. The vouchers may be all right, the accounts balanced and audited; but in the course of the official year things have happened not set down in them, which will have to be squared by some sharp thrusts, some sly insinuation or open accusation. Sometimes an order or motion is proposed that proclaims somebody is to be punished; nothing is said, but everyone knows what it means; and there is a silent relish in the rustic bosom, at seeing a neighbor, especially if he happens to be in office, made uncomfortable. Meanwhile, the cross-questioning goes on, with an occasional speech by some citizen, whose only opportunity it is in the course of the year. The motion is about to be put; suddenly the gentleman from Clamshell Corner and Battle Alley springs to his feet and says he is not ready for the question. He takes a wide range; condemns the way in which almost everything has been managed the year past, and offers much sage and angry counsel; which, having relieved himself of, his good nature returns, he faces about, votes as usual, and for half a year is a partisan of the authorities. But Mr. Toothacher, from Jerry's Pint and Outalong, is a more steady-going opponent of every board of selectmen; his general view is that the town's affairs are going to the dogs. He makes no speeches, but he prophecies to a neighbor across the pasture bars, and warms his sarcasms beside the stove of the village store. He is always a thorn in the sides of the selectmen. He wants what he calls a plain statement; he thinks the selectmen have spent too much money; the taxes are ever too much; the roads are good enough for him; the schoolhouse will last another year, and his face is set like flint against all improvements. He is in great contrast to the class who are always ready to vote away other people's money.

Then there is the alien citizen — I mean, not born in New Castle — who is apt to be of liberal tendencies respecting public affairs. His position is difficult. There is the same distinction here between the native born and the alien, as there was in

New Castle Interior

Athens or Rome. Residence is nothing; unless of local descent you find yourself always on the outside of the autocthonous circle and your disabilities unremoved. It is in vain to explain to your fellow-citizens that it was not your fault but misfortune that you were not born in New Castle. Their difficulty is in understanding how this could have happened; and your actually being here is, if not suspicious, always a mystery.

It often happens that the poll-tax is arrayed against the property-tax. Then you will see, on the final vote, the right hand of the younger men, stretched upward full length, in its bold, moneyless freedom, always affirmative, and nearly always triumphant; while the hands of the opposition, the conservative, older citizens, are raised timidly only from the elbow. We can leave them to fight it out on this line; their freedom is safe in their own hands. The town methods of conducting business are clumsy, absurd, informal; the manners of the meeting, rough; now violent, now indifferent; matters proceed confusedly; but the ends attained are the pride of our civilization, equitable taxation, safe roads and bridges, care of the poor, public order and equal and sufficient education for all.

There was a period in the history of all New England towns when they had the care of religion. At length, when divisions in religious sentiment arose, the towns wisely relinquished this care. In New Castle, the right of suffrage did not depend upon church membership; yet, as elsewhere, the church was the power that controlled and gave direction to all civil affairs. Here, the town and church did not become wholly separated until about 1825–30.

That the ancient town-meetings were much like the modern, has been evident to me from careful reading of the records. It is clear enough when matters are in contention; it is clear what is of public interest from year to year. Often you can read between the lines. When a new minister is to be called, the town clerk's record is eloquent with circumlocutions; when it is in discussion whether to build a parsonage, his report shows the prevailing sentiment. In times of trouble, he becomes scriptural; then you may know danger is ahead. Just before the war of 1812, the warrant for a town-meeting calls upon the citizens to bring in their votes " for a person qualified and suitable to represent said town at the legislature for wise men — men skilled in the times, to know what Israel ought to do." Later on, a town clerk stops in his record to exclaim against the corruption of the age; and again to give in full the etymology of the word Federal.

The first town-clerk of New Castle, by election, was Theodore Atkinson. Below are given his signature and seal, used upon official documents.

The constable was the most important town functionary; he collected the rates, and looked after the peace and good order of the people. The seal below is a curious monogram of Rich. Jose, sheriff of the Province and town, in latter part of the seventeenth century. There was a regular night-watch for all parts of the town; and every night the constable, with four men of the watch, visited all public houses to enforce the regulations concerning them. No strangers were allowed in New Castle above fourteen days, without notice to the selectmen. Whoever sold liquor to a common drunkard was liable to fine; and the selectmen gave to the inn-keeper the names of persons to whom they were forbidden to sell. An excellent regulation.

The first regular town-meeting, held according to the time fixed by the charter, was 6th March, 1694. In the same year, in

October, the first assembly-men were chosen, — Thomas Cobbet and James Randel. The expenses of the second year of the town's existence were £22 6s 3d. In them were included the cost of copying the charter and the parchment for the same, and also the cost of the very book on which are written these first accounts and records. From year to year were added the various other officers for administering local affairs, as the need arose; as justices of the peace, highway surveyors, cullers of staves, packers of mackerel and meats, hog-reeves, fence-viewers, pound-keepers, tythingmen, criers and sextons. School-committees were not yet. Assembly-men were chosen at special meetings, by a prescript from the governor and council. Their pay was about three dollars per day; they sat sometimes for a day, never longer than two weeks, and adjourned to fixed dates; until dissolved by the same authority which had called them together.

The greatest trial laid upon the town authorities of New Castle, in the first years of its incorporation, was the "seating of the meeting-house." To draw the social line across square pews, side seats and galleries, and please everybody, was as difficult as to arrange a modern procession, or dinner-table. In 1695, the town decided to inflict penalties upon such as did not comply with the orders in regard to where they should sit in the meeting-house.'

In 1695, the expenses had swelled to £118 6s 9d; but the larger part of it was to meet the Province tax and the salary of the minister. The next year, 1696, occurs the most important item of information contained in the old records; it is an inventory of estates and ratable persons in New Castle; the ratable estates returned amounted to £1115 11s, heads ratable, 108. This would give a population of about 500, and a respectable average of property.

I will give here a copy of the original prescript for the town-meeting of this year, 1696:

"These are to give notice to the Freeholders and inhabitants of this town that they are to meet at the meeting-house at eight of the clock in ye morning, on Tuesday come sennight, it being the first Tuesday in M'ch for to choose constables, selectmen and other officers for this town acc'd to a charter granted by the Right Hon. John Usher, Esq. Lieut. Gov. & Comm. in Chief of this Province."

How much more like a city government was the ancient board of selectmen than it now is, may be seen in the custom, formerly, of a monthly meeting, to attend to any business brought before it. The selectmen sat as judges, deciding trivial matters appertaining to the community. As many of our early selectmen were also members of the Provincial government, all their actions had great weight and dignity. The citizens might naturally expect that the interests of the town, in its relations with the Province, would not suffer. The selectmen, for some time after the incorporation of New Castle, held their monthly meetings at the house of Dame Hannah Purmont, whom I have mentioned before as the popular hostess of her time. I will quote some specimens of the kind of business transacted there by our selectmen at their monthly meetings:

"Marjorie Roe being complained of for her not taking care to maintain herself, was sent for before the selectmen; and she was then ordered by the selectmen to put herself upon some honest employment whereby to maintain herself within one month's time — or she should be sent unto ye town whence she came."

"Ordered · that any person that lives in any dwelling house in this town shall provide to the said house a good ladder; it shall reach to the top of said house."

"Ordered · that whoever letts their chimney take fire that it flames out at ye top, unless in the time of snow or rain, and then set on fire on purpose, shall pay the sum of 10s for each default."

"Ordered · that no ram be let run on the commons from June 20th until Nov. 1st, on penalty of the loss of the ram, the ram to be killed and divided, one half for the use of the poor and one half to the informer."

They also issued orders in regard to buildings, when they deemed them unsafe or improperly constructed. Lean-tos were their aversion, and they are constantly ordering them to be pulled down. [The lean-to has always been a favorite kind of addition to New Castle houses and barns. The word is pronounced to this day "*lenty.*"]

After a time, the power of the selectmen decreased, and all those matters, like the above, were discussed and decided in open meetings of the citizens. Probably the selectmen had given frequent offence, and exceeded their power. The town now voted to warn the lazy and profligate; to grant licences: to impound

stray hogs: and in general to provide for all its wants, and forearm against all dangers.

Here are examples of the minute care the community exhibited for its own interests: one of which indicates sufficiently well the *paternal* nature of the town government:

"Voted: the Hogs go without yokes in this town the Ensueing Season, except when there may be a complaint of there being very breechy."

"Voted: £25, old tenor, to provide a sufficient Bull in the town the Ensueing year."

Here is an order in regard to the drones of the hive:

"Voted: that the Selectmen have an Enspection over ye Inhabitants of ye Town, and wherein they find them Lasey as they do live, they See that they may be imployed and put to work."

Our records contain the epitome of our history; but less and less circumstantial as time goes on. I have no intention of giving a documentary history; it would require a volume by itself. It would be a work which I should praise, as critics do, without reading. I but glance at such portions as are entertaining and characteristic: prototypes of men and manners, with which I am more or less familiar to-day; but which, ignorant of their antecedents, would be hard to understand.

New Castle continued its career after incorporation, in peace and moderate prosperity, until the Revolution. Schools were established early in the eighteenth century, which grew in public favor continually; schoolhouses were built, money always raised easily, and they were kept open for the larger portion of the year. Sampson Sheafe was the first schoolmaster whose name I find; he was a graduate of Harvard College in 1735. Schools were for boys; girls had small opportunities for education at the public expense. After a time, girls had a school of their own in the summer; then they were admitted to the same schools as the boys, but not until the latter had had the lion's share: that is, the boys were dismissed at four o'clock in the afternoon, and the girls took what was left of the day and the teacher. In time, they had equal privileges; yes, greater, or availed themselves more carefully of them; until it is a common observation that they are better scholars than the boys. Navigation, a favorite study here, was generally taught, not in school, but by some retired ship-master. The compactness of New

Castle has made possible graded schools; a very great advantage, not usual in small country communities. We now have three: primary, intermediate and grammar.

I doubt if the population of the town has varied much for two hundred years; it has seldom been less than five, or more than seven hundred. In 1696, there were 108 ratable men in New Castle; in 1728 there were 131 tax-payers. The first official census after that of 1696 (which only numbered ratable persons) was in 1773. The population was then 601: males, 299; females, 289; slaves, 13.* During the Revolution, the population dwindled to less than 300; but in 1790 had recovered to 534, and at that date there were about one hundred houses. In 1834, there

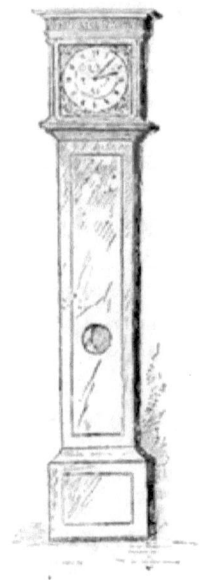

were 150 legal voters, among whom were 14 Amazeens, 7 Bells, 10 Frosts, Lears and Meloons 2 each, 9 Tarltons, 10 Vennards, 16 Whites and 11 Yeatons. According to a private enumeration, made this year by my friend, Mr. Fred. Bell, the inhabitants number 600, and the houses 136.

---

* The writer had the pleasure of discovering, in one of the lumber rooms of the Congressional Library, the original returns of the New Hampshire census of 1773.

In its earlier history, New Castle had always educated men in its midst, and filling its town offices. Theodore Atkinson, graduated at Harvard College in 1718, succeeded his father, of the same name, as town clerk. One of its most prominent citizens, George Jaffrey, sent his son to Cambridge, and, subsequently, a grandson of the same name. All three filled various Provincial offices, as well as being prominent in local affairs.

We give an excellent copy of a portrait of the first George Jaffrey, by Smibert. And also the Jaffrey coat of arms, and the old Jaffrey clock, first set up in the Jaffrey cottage, in 1676, and still numbering the weary hours of its two hundred and eighth year. It is claimed to be the second oldest clock of its kind in the country.*

For the geology of this island, I must refer my reader to the State Report, in three volumes; which may give him the necessary information, though I cannot find it. It is clear, the island is founded on granite of an ancient order, which has been rent and beautified by volcanic dykes.

But we are not without our practical geologist in New Castle. The science, and our poetry of ledges, he knows nothing of; yet he knows what is in them, and how to open them and find it. He is an artist in stone walls; the many-angled, misshapen rocks fall into place and line from his hand, and immediately look as though they could go nowhere else; try to change them and you find it is no fancy, but fact; they are in their appointed places, and fit as if somewhere, and once before, a perfect whole. My friend, William Trefethen, descended from the first of those famous families — Tre, Pol and Pen — of Cornishmen, is the man who can work these stony miracles in a manner much superior to that of the ancient Lithobolus of New Castle. He somewhat resembles the ledges in appearance, scarred and weather-beaten. He is cut out, as we say in the country, for his work. He much magnifies the drill and the blast; and all who do not understand that business, are to him unimportant people. He pretends the ledges know him and are afraid of him, but that they will bully any other man in town; and it is true, he has so identified

---
* I am indebted to Dr. B. Joy Jeffries, of Boston, for permission to copy the portrait; and to Walter Jeffries, Esq., of the same place, for the Jaffrey coat of arms and clock.

The motto of the coat of arms is, *Post Nubila Phœbus.*

himself with them that no one thinks of attacking them without his aid and counsel. He is their true poet and lover. He drills, blasts and pries, and talks to the flying fragments as if they were his children and pets. Everybody runs away from them; he walks leisurely off. He stands to his gun and is never hit. The pieces know him, as the bees their keeper. He declares that a ledge likes to be blown up, is glad of release, of a new sensation and a little travel. This rough and rocky man is a true poet in his relation to the one thing that interests him; and of him we learn geology and, perchance, other useful lessons.

The soil of New Castle is mostly disintegrated rock. This gives to leaf and flower, with the iodine of the sea, their brighter colors than those of inland meadow and mountain. Here, the wild rose in summer is our most abundant and pretty flower; and in autumn the golden-rods, of which there are several kinds. "Plentie of single damask roses, very sweete"— was one of the first descriptive accounts of this part of New England, by Francis Higginson, in 1629. So they continue to be; and everywhere the sweet-briar is mingled with them, tall, delicate, the high-born lady of all wild flowers; suffused, not with the crimson hues of garden roses, but the faint, pink blush of finer blood. Both are single-leaved and full of thorns, difficult to transplant and fading quickly when plucked, the very embodiment of wildness. Go by them, mademoiselle, and leave them where they grow; they cannot adorn your bosom so much as they do your pathway. It is evident they love to be admired, for they gather by all our roadsides and lanes, where they bloom from June to October, the later flowers being always more deeply colored than the earlier, in harmony with the ripened, deeper tone which pervades all nature at the close of the year. The first flower that appears above our ledges is the saxifrage. It bears a cluster of dull, white blossoms, with a faint, sweet perfume. Suddenly they fade and are gone, flower, stem and leaf. It is a very humble plant, yet the boldest I know; for no weather or belated spring intimidates it. It keeps its appointment, evidently, with some stars, whose clustered, milky-way it resembles more than anything in nature, as it covers the bare tops of the ledges, which rise at intervals through the green fields; and in the night you may follow their line by the cloudy whiteness of the thickly-growing saxifrage. The day we look for it we are apt to find it; doubtless it was expecting us; and we now feel, by its sign, that spring cannot be taken away from us.

The latest blooming, of the smaller flowers on this island, is the purple gerardia. "Once, in a golden hour," I tried to bind these two plants into a single nosegay, and gather their spiritual meaning.

ROSE-GERARDIA.

On my small farm where rocks and weeds contend
Which shall possess the most its barrenness,
In earliest spring, the earliest flower,
Almost untimely, is the Saxifrage,
The season's dear though humble harbinger,
Most dear to country folks because the first;
Rearing on fragile stem its clustered crown,
Between the seams of rocks, by east winds blown,
And with a feeble root and few, low leaves
As if it needed neither earth nor sun,
But grew by that exhilarating sense
Of winter past and far-off breath of spring
That likewise man by his own tokens knows.
But when all summer's lush and favored flowers,
Fed on the highest suns and richest dews,
Rooted in mellow soil and sheltered nooks,
Are blighted with the year's autumnal change,
Then once again, in thin, unfertile lands,
Along the beach-side, and the meadow marge,
The Rose-Gerardia swings its little bell,
And will not let the season go too soon,
But holds it with a blessing and a tear.
Its very leaves do deprecate the frost,
Already brown so not to tempt his touch.
And as the thought of spring, and not spring's self,
Drew from its crevices along the ledge
The sweet, presaging herald, Saxifrage,
So now the latest flower, on winter's verge,

Grows by the memory of summer days,
Dreams of the rose and blushes at its dream.

All of the more common wild flowers are found here; I know of no rare ones. Stramonium grows on the beaches; the wild pea also, and wild celery. There grows also the single-plumed, sea-side golden-rod. The wild morning-glory, convolvulus or man-of-the-earth,* is common and luxuriant. Violets, both white and blue, the fields are full of in May and June, but without odor. Columbine is found on ledges where there is a little soil. The wood anemone we have, but not arbutus, which is singular, considering the situation, and that it is found everywhere else in the region. Perhaps the island was not Puritanic enough for the may-flower of the Pilgrims. Our white daisies are uncommonly large; they are the beautiful pests of all our grass-lands. The purple asters seldom stray into our fields, but keep to the road-sides, in company with golden-rods, roses and low lambkill. Clethra, or sweet-pepperbush, I have never found but once. Pyrola, or winter-green, Indian-pipe, pinesap, are rare. Here and there is a shadbush, and catkinned willows are common. The water-willows show signs of renewing life, in damp weather, as early as February. We have the most beautiful of the orchis tribe, the adder's-tongue pogonia. The pimpernel is not very common here; we find it oftenest in the bottom of old cart-tracks through the fields nearest the shore. The cranberry springs up on the sides of every wet place and in all the swamps. Once we thought the cranberry would make us so comfortable that we could cultivate the muse at ease, upon its profits. What mud, sand and roots did we do battle with in right good will! In vain: and this little, red, acid grape of the swamp we now look upon in the temper of Æsop's fox. But for one thing we still commend it: no amount of cultivation ever deprives it of its wild flavor. There is a single small patch of the mountain cranberry on the island, an estray from some distant hill-top. I could name several other plants, not indigenous here, but which I have seen for a single season and no more. There are many beautiful wild grasses, which, in like manner,

---

* The convolvulus has a root, increasing in size and stumpy at the end, and a fancied resemblance to a little man.

come and go, failing to find a friendly habitat. Sooth to say, there is one we have always with us; though we drive it to the edge of the field, we never get it quite out; it comes back under ground, secretly forcing its way with many-jointed, sharp-pointed spears; it is what we name here witch-grass, miscalled from quitch-grass; known to some as couch-grass, and in botany as *triticum repens*. It is a very good grass for lazy farmers, since the land will yield a fair crop of hay from it, after every other kind has run out.

The most common shrubs are the bayberry, barberry and sweet-fern. The barberry, which Jeremy Belknap says had become domesticated here as early as 1792, is a handsome object among the rocks all the year round. Its root and inner bark, of bright yellow, are much used by New Castle dames for dyeing. Its fruit hangs upon the sprays all winter; which, with the great crimson panicle of the sumach, lights up December days, or warms the snowy landscape. Besides this beauty, it has a use: many a poor robin and sparrow, belated, or having lost their southern way, save themselves from starvation on the dried seeds of the barberry. Therefore, you who are mindful of your own winter sauce, remember the hungry little birds, and do not quite strip the bushes. When very hard pushed, birds will eat the juniper berry, which is about as large, and full as bitter, as any pill. When I see the crows eating them I know there is absolute distress and famine in their world. The juniper is providential in the worst seasons to the mice, also, who find under its warm blanket unfrozen ground, and, not infrequently, eat up their benefactor.

I think it was Thoreau who said in his rambles on Cape Cod, that every landscape which was dreary enough, had a certain beauty to his eyes. The same remark has been made about very homely people. Excessive sand or rock have their own charm; which here the juniper adds much to. It quickly covers all waste, unsightly places, with its green, charitable mantle. The universal effort of nature is toward beauty. If the earth is an accident; it has had remarkable luck to make itself so perfect and so admirable as to conceal its base origin, and seem like a premeditated work of the highest skill. But let us not trouble ourselves with theology or science; both are robbers; one of our peace of mind, the other of our admiration, to which there ever goes something of mystery. One small fairy field in New Castle is worth the whole kingdom of science.

Closely akin to the juniper is the savin-tree, which, though an evergreen, wears in winter a brownish dress. I am not sure that the creeping juniper is not occasionally overtaken with an ambition to become a tree, and that it masquerades, like a successful parvenu, in the form of a savin, now and then. It is not, however, very triumphant here, rarely reaching a height of over eight feet; and it pays the penalty of its presumption by an early death.

Of deciduous trees we have almost none. Certain parts of the island were once sparsely covered with oak and walnut, which, by the end of the Revolution, had mostly disappeared. Their wood may now be found in many an old New Castle house. The original growth of hard-wood trees was used up in house and boat building, and in various fortifications constructed here from 1640 to 1776, and for fuel. Subsequently the town was dependent for fuel upon peat, of which large quantities used to be dug out of the swamps; and upon wood, brought in gundalows from the shores of the creeks and the upper Piscataqua. At all times the beaches have furnished driftwood and timber, and often more valuable prizes. "Chipping" is a favorite employment of women and children; and anything too large for a basket is left to be called for with a boat. You can always find enough to boil the summer tea-kettle. An old sea-log, well soaked and salted, makes the best of backlogs; the best because it lasts long, hardly burns, but, as it were, simmers, with here and there little tongues of bright yellow and green flames. With some dryer and more combustible sticks from the wood-pile, you may kindle a cheerful blaze, and in the long winter evenings stretch your legs before it, and

—"let the grey-green sea
Go tumble as it will upon the shore."

As you sit and look into the drift-wood fire, and see how the deadest log can be made lively, you readily believe the Indian's book of Genesis, which said that the first pair were created out of drift-wood. The miracle can be repeated; at least open fires are favorable in bringing to life the affections and human attractions.

Pines now cover all the uncultivated portions of New Castle. Long may they soar and sing!

> — "argutumque nemus pinosque loquentes
> Semper habet."

But the wood-dealer looks with envious eye upon them. We have just now plucked, as brands from the burning, the pines of Bos'n Hill. There are three kinds of them here: the white, pitch or yellow, and the Norway pine, known also, popularly, as the stone-pine. The white-pine is four-leaved, the pitch three-leaved, and the Norway two-leaved.

> "In strict society
> Three conifers, white, pitch and Norway pine,
> Five-leaved, three-leaved and two-leaved, grow hereby."

The pine woods shelter us very much from the cold, northwesterly winds of winter; and their wholesome balsam fills the summer air. They also make a fine harmony of color, against the gray, protruding ledges and the sea.

The earth does not cease to produce infinite forms of life when it sinks out of sight and the ocean covers it. To the very verge of the tide grow the things which love the sun and the upper air; and, at the next step, begins another order of beings, vegetable and animal, living in the vespertinal light of the under world. We dwell here on the boundary of these two realms, and have to deal with both.

The emblem of New Castle should be a waving line.

As the land approaches the sea it prepares itself for the plunge; becomes more and more naked, in order to support those forms of life that need only the bare rock.

The fortunes of New Castle would make an excellent subject for a novel or poem; they continually divert one from writing exact history, which, however completely explored and related, would be unimportant, and of interest only to those already interested. I have aimed at a larger audience in treating of what is characteristic in an insular people, and their peculiar environment. This people has undergone many strange fortunes from political events, and from the accident of their situation.

Though never having seen much actual conflict, they have been continually in a state of preparation and alarm. They were in dread of French and Indians from the first settlement almost to the Revolution. In the beginning of the latter war, they lost their homes and much of their property. New Castle was nearly deserted in the winter of 1775; such as remained lived in their cellars, from fear of the attack of British cannon. The town was pillaged by the enemy, and damaged almost as much by our own troops. For the latter loss it was granted recompense to the amount of nearly one thousand pounds. After the Revolution the times were hard; the depreciated currency would buy but little, and there was little to buy; while whoever held on to his paper money was liable to be ruined. In January, 1780, it took fifteen dollars to pay for one bushel of corn; by August of the same year, fifty. Beef, at the same date, was worth four and one-half dollars per pound; and leather six to twenty dollars per pound. No sooner had the town recovered from the misfortunes of this war, than it was again disturbed and made to suffer for full four years by the war of 1812. And though there was prosperity here during the Rebellion, it was only apparent; it was harmful, and it left behind evils. The government works here, and the Navy Yard near by, might seem to be an advantage for laboring men and mechanics; yet the effect has been to debauch the political conscience of this community, as of all others in the neighborhood. The Navy Yard has been, in particular, the source of the most dangerous kind of social evils; indirect bribery in elections; larger wages, shorter hours and less work in them, than private enterprise could compete with; withdrawal of men from their trades and natural occupations, until they became unfitted for them, and incapable of any effort while the Navy Yard held out a prospect, for which they were willing to wait in idleness and expectation half a year for a month's job, — in short, preferring the government's half loaf to any other whole. This has been the danger to independence of thought in politics, and the obstruction to material prosperity.

Other kinds of adversity the town has not known much of. No great fire has ever occurred; and but one deadly pestilence, — that was in 1735, and it swept over the whole Province. New Castle lost eleven children, among other deaths, under ten years of age, in a few days. It was called a "throat distemper," and, at the time, attributed "to some occult quality in the air." No doubt it was a diphtheritic epidemic.

Two memorable storms have devastated the island, on its eastern, northern and southern sides. On the 22d February, 1683, happened the fiercest storm and highest tide ever known on the New England coast up to that period. The bridge across Little Harbor was nearly ruined in this storm. It was the time, already described, of the comet, of Cranfield, of witchcraft, and the minds of men in this region, at least, were filled with distress. In April, 1851, occurred the next great storm, the effects of which are still visible in New Castle. It began on a full moon, spring tide, and the wind blew a gale three days and nights from the northeast. The sea broke through the beaches, and made an island of Jaffrey Point. People gathered their household goods together, ready to depart on the third day to some friendly Ararat. Some thought it the end of all things, and prepared to face it where they were. It is very difficult to remember the scriptural promise of no more floods, when a great storm comes down on the seashore at the equinoxes. Once already, according to Indian tradition, has the human race been destroyed in New Hampshire by a watery catastrophe; and re-peopled by a single pair, a Chief Powaw and his squaw, who saved themselves on the top of Mt. Washington. We have this hope and security therefore: we can flee to the hills in the last emergency, with a faint chance of founding a new and better race.

There were several years of scarcity in the earlier history of this Province, and also during the present century, which I notice only to observe how the people of this island were enabled to weather them,—how, in fact, they have under whatever fortunes, maintained themselves, from the beginning until to-day. It has been by fish and the fishing interest. The years 1814–15–16 were years of scarcity; the crops failed; corn was two dollars and fifty cents per bushel, and pork twelve dollars and fifty cents per hundred weight. Seed corn was difficult to obtain. Again, in 1837, there was a year of almost famine. But in all these years of want, it was noticed that the mackerel came close in shore, so that everybody obtained a supply, enough for the winter and some to exchange for necessities. Thus the hand of Providence, not only has supported this people in distress, by a direct interposition, but has by the same token pointed out to them plainly their proper business and vocation. It has shown them why they were planted in the midst of the seas; nor has it, as yet, by any divine signal, called them from their beautiful home and appointed work, to become apostles and prophets. It is enough to be a skipper in summer, and a grand-juryman in winter.

Whatever fails they can go a-fishing. Though money be scarce, nothing doing at the Navy Yard, no shoes to make, no earthworks building and the world likely to last another year, there are still treasures in the sea for the seeking. The fisherman can almost always secure a share of them; so that he can sell some, some he can cure for future use, and the remainder is food for the day. And the fisherman is ever expecting a prize; expectancy is his flag, and an undying hope his chart: these make of his business a half pastime.

The fisherman's idyl has never been written.* His life remains such as it has been, with little variation, in all ages; and here for more than two hundred years there has been no marked change, and few of those improvements and inventions which in the same period have transformed nearly all other trades and pursuits. Such pictures, such activity and events as belonged to these shores and their inhabitants long ago may be observed to-day.

The spring has come; the fishermen are seen about their vessels and boats, bending sails, scraping spars and masts, patching and painting. They are preparing for a cruise, and soon are uneasy to be off. They wait a day or two longer for weather, for bait, or something to complete the outfit. Now the "Mary Eliza" is presumed to be as nearly ready as all hands can make her. I see, over the low hills and the village roofs, her slender masts swaying with the turning tide. She is all in order, tidy, provisioned and ballasted; and early in the morning, yes, at midnight, the skipper is aboard, and the older men of the crew arrive not long after; they begin to trim the sails; they are waiting for the young men, whom perchance their sweet-

---

* Theocritus attempted one, but not with his usual success. The fish itself has had better luck, though never equal to that of the bird's. Yet fine, poetic words have been written in praise and description of fish; and St. Anthony's sermon to them is almost a poem.

: Newcastle Fishermen :

hearts' arms are delaying. Now the crew is numbered; the mooring cast off. She takes the tide around Fort Point and Stileman's Rocks; the wind is still asleep; the sun, bringer of the soft morning breeze, is not up; though Whale's Back Light begins to pale against the morning red. In the far east the sun is suddenly born, large, amorphous, with no splendor in his beams as yet. But the wind of the west springs up at the same moment, brightening his face, filling the sails of the little vessel almost instantly. Now she gains way and obeys the helm to an inch. She glides past Whale's Back, past Kitt's Rock, and takes the wind on the other quarter, steering eastward. She has entered upon her voyage in earnest. We watch her with heartfelt goodwill; from the cliff waves a white handkerchief; it signals a deeper emotion than ours. But our wish is common — may they all return that go forth, and with a full fare! She has become a speck on the great ocean; when you take your eyes from her now you will not be able to find her again.

www.ingramcontent.com/pod-product-compliance
Lightning Source LLC
Chambersburg PA
CBHW021824230426
43669CB00008B/854